THE MAKING OF
ISRAEL

By the same author

THE MAKING OF
ISRAEL

James Cameron

Taplinger Publishing Company
New York

First published in the United States in 1977 by
TAPLINGER PUBLISHING CO., INC.
New York, New York

Library of Congress Catalog Card Number: 77–76041
ISBN 0 8008 5084 X

Sources of Photographs

Associated Press 8, 18, 24–33, 36, 40, 43, 49, 57–97; Black Star 3; Camera Press 6/7, 9, 12, 22; Popperfoto 21, 56; Radio Times Hulton Picture Library 14–17, 34, 35, 41, 52, 98.

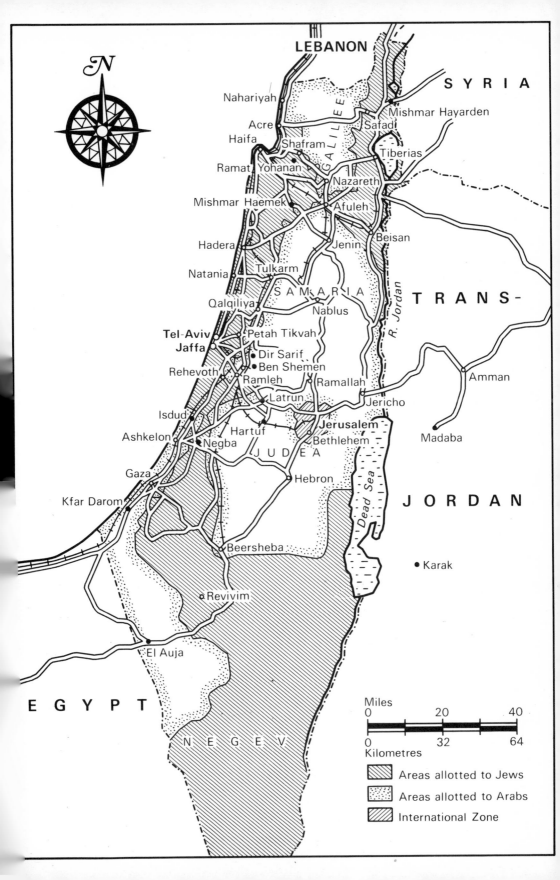

FOREWORD

This is an account – not *the* account – of the last days of Palestine, and the first hours of Israel.

In trying to picture in so few words the climax of a conflict of such sad and wearisome complexity I am only too conscious of the inevitable oversimplifications, the omissions, possibly the mistakes. The whole history of the Middle East has been a tragedy of errors; it would be strange if details in the record escaped. But everything in this short book is true, as far as a score of people's memories can be true, including my own.

'The introduction of the Jewish State into the Arab heartland exalted many hearts and broke many more. More than anything in this century it was at once a triumph and a desolation. Full of high hopes, it produced the most intractable conflict of our times...' I wrote that for this book and, no matter what ensues between then and now, that at least must remain true. I accept the impossibility of keeping pace with this feverishly volatile history; that is not my intention. I am writing of a generation ago.

No man nor woman I know can be truthfully objective about the Palestine question. Between the historian and the propagandist of our generation lurks a very misty frontier.

I was there – not continually but at intervals – during the period described here. In the quarter-century of Israel's existence I came to know it very well. With the exception of the 1973 campaign I

1

was involved in all its wars. I have equally seen the sorrowful frustrations of the refugees they created.

Nevertheless the newborn Israel of the 50s and 60s was a place of excitement and exhilaration for me; as a non-Jew I rejoiced and shared in its optimism. Many of the events following the Six-Day War distressed and dispirited me; it seemed the Israelis were capable of anything, except promoting their cause in the eyes of others.

Now that Israel both deserves and requires to be treated no longer as a fledgling but as a nation among nations, I have not changed my mind in either respect.

The Second World War had ended, but not for the British forces policing what had for thirty years been the Mandate of Palestine. Up until the very last day of the occupation the soldiers maintained and demonstrated their authority, patrolling the roads in armoured cars, harassed to the last by snipers. As the end of the Mandate's days approached, no serious attempt could be made to hold the ring between Jews and Arabs. The show of force became more and more symbolic.

ONE

At half-past eleven that night the British naval flotilla began to move out into the darkness from the Bay of Haifa, in what was to be for half an hour more the land of Palestine. A screen of destroyers and frigates surrounded the flagship, the carrier *Ocean*, followed by the cruiser *Euryalus*, carrying aboard the departing British High Commissioner. By and by we saw the ships' searchlights trained on the flagship; a guard of honour was assembled on the flight-deck. The retreat was to be effected in the Royal Naval fashion, that is to say with some style, and a certain graceful arrogance.

At midnight exactly they reached the limits of Palestine's territorial waters. In *Euryalus* the High Commissioner mounted the bridge and saluted the flagship. The guard of honour presented arms while the band played 'God Save the King' and then, with the British sense of sentimental irony, 'Auld Lang Syne'. *Euryalus* sailed on westwards, bearing Sir Alan Cunningham to Malta, and Palestine into limbo.

The British Mandate had ended, and the State of Israel was born.

That was the 14th of May 1948, or the 5th of Iyar in the Jewish calendar of the year 5708.

This was of course far from the beginning of the story and, unfortunately, far from the end. Twenty-six years and four wars later the end had still not come, might never come. The introduction of the Jewish State into the Arab heartland exalted many hearts and broke many more. More than anything in this century it was at once a triumph and a desolation. Full of high hopes, it produced the most intractable conflict of our times. The Israelis were soon to find that no man is an island, however desperately he might wish his isolation, and the Powers who had begotten the new land, or opposed it, mostly in their own interests, were to learn that something had happened in the Middle East far greater than could have been foreseen on that night of May in 1948. The story of Israel – as it was in the beginning, and is now – has been one of eternal transition from the good to the bad, and the bad to the good, and back again, and yet again. Only those of us who shared its birth-pangs in 1948 believed – innocently, as we all now know – that we had been witness to an act of creation.

Every Israeli story began with the words: 'Now, after 2,000 years...' The early days of the State produced a variant: 'For the first time in 2,000 years an article has appeared in the Hebrew Press that does not begin: "For the first time in 2,000 years..."' The poignancy was that it was all the truth, back in the days when *Euryalus* carried away the last of the British power and left the Promised Land to David Ben-Gurion and the Yishuv. It was the redemption of an exile that had begun when Moses led his tribesmen from bondage in Egypt into Canaan, through the destruction of Judea by the Romans in the first century of the Christian era and the flight of the Jews into the Diaspora. In a context like this there can be nothing to add to the excellent reportage in the books of the Old Testament and the works of Josephus.

Yet the creation, or invention, of the State of Israel – probably the most twentieth-century of all nationalisms – simply cannot be comprehended in its dedicated and almost sublime impertinence without immersion in the history of which it was the culmination. If the concept is sentimental, as it is, and romantic, as it is, and indeed anguished, as it is, and if today's *Realpolitik* has turned a fairytale into the barrel of a gun, nevertheless it cannot be forgotten that it began in a legend – probably the most concrete and businesslike piece of mythology of our times, yet still somehow born from an act of faith. For fifty generations the incantation of the

5

Orthodox had always been: 'Next year in Jerusalem'. Before that pious (and some said pompous) prayer could even come into realisable hope there had to be the holocaust of Hitler, the brutal climax of all the world's latent anti-Semitism, and the destruction of six million Jews. 'Next year in Jerusalem' had to await 'Last year in Dachau'. Adolf Hitler was the Founding Father of the Land of the Jews.

*Jewish immigration into Palestine was still
strictly controlled by the White Paper of 1939 to
1,500 a month. Inevitably this brought about the
Aliyah Beth – the traffic in illegal immigrant
ships, old chartered vessels from everywhere in
the Mediterranean and the Black Sea, some
barely seaworthy, grossly overcrowded, hoping
somehow to pass unseen into Haifa. Most were
intercepted; many just disappeared. One, the
Exodus was, in an act of barely credible crudity,
actually returned to Germany. This vessel,
crammed to the gunwales with 1,300 immigrants, was lucky; it reached Haifa just three
days before the British left, and was escorted
into harbour.*

No one remembers what this ship was originally called, nor exactly where she came from. She was renamed the Jewish State, *and she arrived too soon. She was boarded by the British soldiers in Haifa harbour, as had been a few hours earlier the* Geulah, *just behind, which had carried 1,500 illegal immigrants.*

A vast piece of history must now be ruthlessly telescoped.

This is not self-indulgence; very much otherwise. A chronicle of the creation of almost any of the forty-odd new post-war States could have started at square one; not so with Israel, an invention that can only make sense through the wrong end of the telescope. Or, some would say, the right end.

For centuries after the Dispersal the seed of Zionism was Messianic and passive: it was accepted that the return of the home-sick Jews must await some sort of divine intervention. As things turned out, this did not look like being a very fruitful attitude politically. The growing enlightenment and liberalism of eighteenth-century Europe disturbed this fatalism. Judaism remained, and remains, essentially tribal. But the French Revolution and the Napoleonic expansion broke down the walls of many ghettoes, and also of many ghetto minds. Philosophers like Moses Mendelssohn and Moses Hess argued that the Jew could join the world and rid himself of his particularism without corrupting his faith, but it was hard to sell that message to a people still faced with serious social and legal discrimination (especially in Russia, so isolated from all the trends of the time) forcing the Jews deeper and deeper behind their protective spiritual barricades. There were still abrupt and horrible pogroms, ancient myths and libels were revived. It did seem, indeed, that anti-Semitism was not just an aberration but endemic to the nature of European man, and part of the permanent social structure of the Jews.

Then came Theodor Herzl. The pre-history of Israel is studded with these seminal names.

Herzl was a cultivated Viennese journalist who had drifted into a life far from his Jewish origins, and who might well have stayed there, but for the Dreyfus case. Captain Alfred Dreyfus, a Jewish officer in the French Army, was framed in 1894 on a greatly publicised treason charge – an obvious scapegoat, as it now appears. Theodor Herzl was outraged: if this sort of thing could happen in France, the one land of civilised and liberal values, what hope could there be for Jews anywhere – outside a Jewish State?

There were of course already Jewish communities in Palestine, but Herzl's idea was far grander: a sovereign *Judenstaat* financed by rich Jewish interests – in a word, the Promised Land physically and economically fulfilled. In 1897 the world's first Zionist Congress met in Basle, aimed 'at establishing for the Jewish people a legally assured home in Palestine'. It got nowhere, naturally. But it did engender Chaim Weizmann.

Chaim Weizmann was less impetuous than the romantic and fiery

Herzl; he believed that Zionism could not be bought by rich sub-ventions but must needs be an organic growth, 'to be watched, nurtured and nursed'. He was just what made so many activists impatient and fretful in years to come: an apostle of the inevitability of gradualness. (For all that, he lived to be the first and perhaps the only memorable President of the State of Israel.)

Dr Weizmann was a most eminent chemist who gave great service to the British Government during the First World War by devising a process for the manufacture of acetone, which makes explosives. It was he who extracted from the then British Foreign Minister – through gratitude, expediency, absent-mindedness, no one will ever know – the famous Balfour Declaration of 1917, in which Arthur Balfour, not unmindful of the need to win over American Jewry to the Allied cause, formally expressed that: 'HM Government view with favour the establishment in Palestine of a national home for the Jewish people.'

It was ambiguous, elusive, provocative, but it was the spring-board. For years thereafter, try as they might, HM Government was never able to wriggle out of it.

To the Arabs the Balfour Declaration was quite simply an act of outright imperialism, in which Britain wilfully disposed of the future of territory to which she had no rightful claim at all, without any consultation whatever with the ninety-two per cent non-Jewish part of the population, a wholly arbitrary colonialist mortgaging of people's lives. To the British it was probably just a parenthetical afterthought in the middle of a dire national emergency. To the Jews of the world it was the green light.

The curtain now drops briefly to denote the passing of thirty-one long and troubled years.

Those who did manage to land in Haifa had only a few hours' grace in the Promised Land before they, too, were sent back to internment. As they went up the gangway to the British troopship that was to take them to Cyprus the Army screened them, to ensure that no one on the wanted list of the Palestine Police was seeking to escape.

TWO

During this interval, however, the scene-shifters are immensely hard at work, and the telescoping of time becomes really drastic. Palestine is no longer a fief of the defeated Ottoman Empire but a British Mandate of the League of Nations. In the first twenty years of the century some half-million Jews have settled in Palestine. They have arrived in definable waves, each called an *aliya* (a word which prosaically means immigration, but which in the Bible means 'ascendance'), all slightly different – urban Jews from Eastern Europe, petit-bourgeoisie knowing nothing of the land and surviving mainly on the bounty of Baron Edmond de Rothschild; working-class fugitives from Russian pogroms; idealists, politicals, professional exiles, socialists, capitalists, fundamentalists, orthodox and heretical, opportunists and dedicated men. From some of these pioneers grew the institutions that became the iron brace of the Jewish land: the *kibbutzim*, the commune-settlements evolved on a vaguely Tolstoyan pattern, in which no wage was paid and all things shared – though this is a simplistic definition; nothing in Israel is as easy as it sounds. Nor can it be denied that the Palestine Arabs were being gradually dispossessed; the Zionist theme had no place in it for a native proletariat.

Aboard the British troopship Empire Rival *a group of Jewish women, frustrated in their attempt to enter Palestine, prepare a meal on their way to internment in Cyprus. They were well fed by the Army, not ill-used; except in that they were refused the one thing they asked for – a home.*

Already this incursion is an alien and disturbing intrusion into the old-established Yishuv of Palestine, the society of pious Jews who spend their lives in devotional study, unworldly and aloof, toiling and spinning not, buried in the arcane interpretations of the Scriptures, sustained by Jewish subventions from abroad, the *Haluka*. The new hard-working and dynamic immigrants despise the *Haluka* and all its associations of alien charity. There are Israelis to this day who regard the massive American patronage of Israel as *Haluka*; there is little they can do about it.

However, before the curtain rises again in our times, the stage-hands are vigorously creating a great transformation-scene. The whole face of Palestine is changing its character. Until 1933 the bulk of the Jewish immigrants have been from Eastern Europe, but in that year the terrible and momentous shadow that had been growing over Germany suddenly assumes the form of a fist; for in Germany the Nazis have come to power. The Fifth Aliya begins – a desperate immigration culturally German, financially German, intellectually German: this corner of the Middle East becomes populated with Herr Doktors and Herr Professors, musicians and artists and lawyers and above all businessmen, all retreating from a bestial and intolerable threat. Germany's loss is Palestine's gain;

in the twenty years until 1939 Palestine absorbs £120,000,000 of Jewish capital. New towns arise, factories appear, more and more land goes into cultivation. The spectacle being assembled behind the curtain is changing in a way that even Theodor Herzl could not have foreseen. Judea is – insidiously, impromptu, *ad hoc*, and, as it turned out, perilously – becoming Jewish despite itself. It is not to the taste of the British governors.

Still less, to be sure, is it to the taste of the existing Arab population of Palestine, nor indeed of all the nations of the surrounding Middle East. By now there was a new member of that company;

The island of Cyprus in the 1940s was a British Colony, and for a while a British concentration-camp. There the illegal Jewish immigrants were confined behind the wire, those who had broken the quota laws of the White Paper issued in 1939, before the German War. They were not abused, they were only enclosed. They were housed under canvas or in huts. From 1940 to 1948 47 ships were intercepted; 65,307 Jews interned.

in 1923 the British had given independence to what was then called Transjordan, under the Hashemite Emir Abdulla, henceforth 'Jordan'. Already the Arabs are watching with a kind of furious fascination the growth of a community of alien Jews whose right to live there rested on a remote ancestral Scriptural title that makes no sense to a Muslim peasant. Moreover, the vast majority of the new Jews had not arrived to take their ease; they work long hours, they build, they invest, they make things grow; it is an energetic lifestyle and an endless challenge to that of the Arabs.

Conflicts grow, fighting spreads all over the land, Palestine becomes an arena of endless guerrilla warfare. Now, behind the curtain, the stage is being set for a very long act. The aspirations of the Jews and the Arabs are irreconcilable; the whole Middle East is on a collision-course. The British Mandate which was to hold the ring is failing, as it was bound to fail, since in its heart it never understood what the struggle was all about. The whole industrial world is now conscious of the immense factor of oil. Both Arabs and Zionists are now a pawn in that game, too.

But before the bell rings for the second act there has to be a Hitler, there has to be a Belsen and an Auschwitz and a Ravensbruck and the delirium of a Second World War. There is, still barely credible, the story of the Final Solution, the death-wagons and the gas-ovens, horribly confirmed when at last the camps are opened up. There have to be the Nuremberg Trials. The world has to be precipitated into an awareness of a Jewish situation it had never contemplated. An unprecedented factor has entered into history: the Collective Conscience.

A Cypriot internment camp was not what they had hoped, but it was better than Dachau, it was better than the immigrant ship. The State of Israel was not yet born, but it would be, one day. After 2,000 years, one could wait awhile.

We have arrived in the post-war world, which as far as Israel is concerned is where most of us came in. Already Britain, the Mandatory Power, had had second and third thoughts about the Balfour Declaration, and the White Paper of 1939 stringently restricted Jewish immigration into Palestine to 1,500 a month. And so began the *aliyah beth*, the illegal immigrant ships bringing desperate Jews from Europe to Palestine, consistently intercepted, frequently just disappearing. In the autumn of 1940 the *Patria* sank with the loss of 250 lives. In February 1942 the *Struma*, with 769 men and women and children, was driven out of Istanbul to blow up, leaving one survivor. So it went on: the *Smyrna*, the *Palmach*, the *San Dimitrio*, the *Hatikva*, the *Mered Haggetoat*. By and by more than 65,000 Jews were in detention camps in Cyprus. Finally, with a stunning impact, the *Exodus*.

Gradually the trickle of immigrants is permitted to move out of the Cyprus camps into Palestine. Five hundred orphaned Jewish children, caged in a transport ship and guarded by British soldiers, leave for home at last.

In July 1947 the *President Warfeld*, an old 1800-ton Mississippi steamer rescued from the scrapyards and renamed *Exodus*, sailed from the South of France for Haifa with 4,550 Jewish men, women, and children, survivors of the death-camps, now refugees from the Displaced Persons' camps in Germany.

The British Navy shadowed it, attacked and rammed it, towed the crippled *Exodus* into Haifa harbour and, to the shocked astonishment of the world, turned these beaten people round and returned them to the hated soil of Germany – an act of gross and almost inexplicable crudity. In the port of Hamburg the refugees were physically dragged ashore and sent back behind the German barbed wire. Mr Ernest Bevin, the British Foreign Minister, stalwart of the British Labour Party, champion of the London dockers, articulator of the aspirations of the working class – who could not cure himself of his dislike of Jews, nor did especially try to do so, dominated by the Arabists who always influenced the thinking of the Foreign Office – cabled an 'expression of my personal appreciation' to the troops who had done this extraordinary thing. Almost every independent newspaper in the world reported the *Exodus* story with almost incredulous horror. Much of what happened in the Mandate thereafter must be considered against this dismal betrayal.

It was probably too much to expect of a decent, insular, obstinate, untravelled and weary old Labour activist like Bevin to appreciate that reconciling the archaic differences of the Levant was something different to settling an industrial dispute in an English dockyard. Emotions were now involved of which Ernest Bevin knew nothing. He responded reasonably to the argument that Britain was not entitled to dispossess the Arab community in Palestine who had after seven centuries a right to believe they lived there. What he and the British Mandate never grasped was that the post-war Jews were not what they had been; the European nightmare had changed all that; it was now survival or nothing, and survival meant what Balfour had, perhaps so casually, promised in 1917. The Jews had gone like lambs to the slaughter in the gas-chambers; in Palestine they could scheme, and resist, and fight.

Meanwhile among the Jewish settlers in Palestine there has grown up a volunteer defence force known as Haganah. Over the years, in some secrecy and based mainly on the kibbutzim, it has assumed the purpose of an army. In 1937 an impatient schism, tired of a wholly defensive role, broke away to form a National Defence Organisation, the Irgun Zwai Leumi. But even the Irgun is not militant enough for some, and one Abraham Stern forms yet another group, even more devoted to direct action, which becomes known as the Stern Gang.

The British police kill Abraham Stern in 1942, but the Gang endures, dedicated to the principle (not, indeed, so far denied) that power comes out of the barrel of a gun.

By the end of the Great War against Germany in Europe the Irgun, led by a Menachem Begin, much to be heard of in years to come, is at war with the British Mandate in Palestine. In 1944 the Stern Gang assassinates Lord Moyne, Minister of State in Cairo, a thing that outrages the British and the Yishuv alike, and for a brief time the Haganah and the British Army join a united front against the gunmen. It will not last long.

By now the activity behind the curtain is becoming frenetic, and from those who are setting the scene for the big act come abrupt and stunning sounds, explosions and gunfire, cries of triumph and calls for pity. Some of the sounds come from as far away as the United States, where American Jewry loudly redeems its conscience at having escaped the Nazis by putting heavy Zionist pressure on the US Government, and gravely vexing poor Harry Truman, whose sympathies for the tormented Jews are up against his new commercial commitments to Saudi Arabia. Now that the German war is over, David Ben-Gurion sends the head of Haganah to round up surplus American arms for the Palestine Jews. Ben-Gurion, by now disenchanted with the broken promises of the Powers, is increasingly Sinn Fein – Ourselves Alone. He warns the Yishuv to make ready for the war to come.

The Haifa oil refinery and Lydda railway-station are blown up, three naval vessels are sunk and railroad lines cut at fifty points. Nine bridges are demolished. Kol Israel, the secret radio, claims the credit from Palmach, the commando spearhead of the resistance forces.*

20

* Both Haganah and the Irgun had illegal radios, widely heard. But there was a group of mainly German Jews of the Aliyah Khadassa, deep conservatives who advocated co-operating with the British. There was a wry story of a meeting of this group at which it was said: 'Brothers, the Haganah has a secret radio. The Irgun has a secret radio. Why should we not have a secret radio?' A member was delegated to instal it. He returned ruefully. 'I cannot do it,' he said. 'The British refuse to give us a licence for a secret radio.'

The refugees in the British transport Nyasa *gather on deck as Haifa approaches. They are from Germany, Poland, Austria. Their good fortune is to have made the quota; they will land legally, hopefully, part of the foundation of a State that has yet to be born.*

Overleaf: *landfall at last, for the fortunate few who were not turned away. Jewish immigrants disembark – now legally – at Haifa, scrutinised by the British, still the Mandatory power. Buses wait to take them to dispersal centres. Life begins.*

Illegal immigration continues, increases. This is a high priority for the Jews, who not only have to find a home for the tens of thousands still rotting in European DP camps, but are most anxious that Independence shall not come to Palestine while they are a minority of only a third of the population. A clandestine network of communications develops; thousands of refugee Jews are embarked from Mediterranean ports in a mad variety of crazy old ships, anything that will float and steer, and delivered by night on the beaches. Those that were intercepted by the British Navy went back to another set of camps in Cyprus.

The Palestine Arab cause is not particularly helped by the fact that its ostensible leader, Haj el-Husseini, the ex-Mufti of Jerusalem, had spent the war in Berlin broadcasting in Arabic for the Nazis.

A kind of desperation sets in. British paratroopers round up almost 3,000 Jews. On a July day in 1946 a load of milk-churns is delivered to the service door of the King David Hotel in Jerusalem, headquarters for both the Military Command and the High Commission. The milkmen are in Arab clothes, but they belong to an Irgun task-force; and the churns contain not milk but high explosive. The bang rocks the city; it blows to bits a whole wing of the building, and kills a hundred people. Some are Arabs, some are Jews; most are British.

The gloves are truly off. A captured Irgunist called Dov Gruner is sentenced to death by the British for an attack on a police station. Shortly afterward Judge Ralph Windham of the Tel-Aviv District Court is kidnapped at gun-point. The High Commissioner threatens to impose martial law unless he is released. Next day Judge Windham is found unharmed; Dov Gruner is hanged nonetheless. Of such wretchedness is the scene being composed as the observers of the world take their places for the climax.

By now it can be assumed that the British, the Mandatory Authority over Palestine, are now in a state of disenchantment, fed-upness and exasperation unprecedented in their hitherto serene Imperial career; they are now dealing with Jewish perversity (as it seems to them) and Arab obstinacy (as they are obliged to recognise), the combination of which is driving the British, whether they like it

The day before, underwater saboteurs had
damaged the British ship Empire Rival with submarine explosives. Now British troops and
Palestine Police search the coastline for hidden
arms and bombs. They use mine-detectors outside a cottage in the fishing village of Sdoth
Yom, 35 miles south of Haifa.

In the countryside of Palestine terrorist activity
mounted daily. The Haifa–Egypt military ex-
press was blown up near Rehevoth; five soldiers
and three civilians were killed. Similarly, Haifa
oil refinery and Lydda railway station were
attacked, three naval vessels sunk, railroad lines
cut at fifty points, nine bridges demolished.
Responsibility was claimed by Palmach, the
commando spearhead of the Jewish resistance
movement.

or not, into a posture of ignominy and odium that is making them appear to the world alternatively futile and tyrannical. No conceivable proposal that suits the Arabs can possibly mollify the Jews, and vice versa. In their long experience of Colonial paternal diplomacy the British have never been handed such a hot potato as this. Mr Attlee's Government wants no more of it, and in 1947 they toss this embarrassment back to whence it came, or as nearly as possible: they return the Palestine Mandate to the United Nations.

At the back of the British official mind the thought lingers that the UN will be able to handle this intractable mess no better than they, and that their lease on Palestine may even now have to be renewed, or even strengthened. Nobody denies with any conviction that the British are encouraging and physically aiding the Arabs to exacerbate the conflict. Zionist ambitions have no longer any usefulness to British foreign policy, and indeed could well threaten them in the Middle East, where the Arab oil-producers must not be antagonised. The Jewish clandestine activities in seeking arms from Czechoslovakia and the approaches to Russia are also ominous. It is therefore of no moment to the Foreign Office in London whether the Arabs are encouraged to liquidate the Zionist State or whether Palestine is thrown into such confusion that the British are asked to return.

The British, however, are making a serious diplomatic miscalculation: they are not reckoning with the powerful pro-Zionist feeling in America, nor with Russia's hope of seizing this splendid opportunity of eliminating British influence in the Middle East. In years to come the irony will be remembered: that if the State of Israel was sponsored by America, it was Russia too that brought it into being.

26

In July 1946 all Jerusalem was rocked by a tremendous explosion, remembered to this day. A group of the Irgun Zwai Leumi activist movement, disguised as Arab milkmen, penetrated the famous King David Hotel, which housed the Political Government Secretariat and the Headquarters of Army Command. They left a vast charge that blew a wing of the hotel to bits, killing a hundred people inside it – some Arabs, some Jews, but mostly British.

By now in the United Nations the orchestra is tuning up for the final act. In November 1947 the General Assembly, after a cliff-hanging vote (in which Britain abstains) has decided on Partition for Palestine. The UN appoints a Special Commission of eleven most oddly assorted improbables: Australia, Canada, Czecho-slovakia, Guatemala, India, Iran, Holland, Peru, Sweden, Uruguay and Yugoslavia. It labours, and brings forth yet another partition plan. Predictably, it is turned down flat by the Arabs. The minutiae of footnotes and frontier adjustments are argued out and fiddled around, but by now it is abundantly and crystal clear that no compromise any mortal man can devise is going to reconcile the Arabs to the legal existence of a Jewish State in the Middle East.

The Palestine Arab High Committee orders a general strike of Arabs throughout Palestine, and violence spreads. The Jewish Agency orders all young Jews to register for 'security service'. Attacks of one side are followed by counter-attacks of the other. On Christmas Day more than a hundred Arabs and Jews are killed. So it goes on.

The war is now on, and its hub is of course Jerusalem. Jerusalem is embattled and besieged, its Jews wholly dependent on supplies from Tel-Aviv convoyed through the Arab-held hills. (Its approach roads are still littered – deliberately and as monuments – with the debris of the trucks that did not get through.)

The Jewish Irgun strikes back savagely, taking the village of Deir Yassin and killing 254 of its men, women and children. This brings the growing terror of the Palestine Arabs to a climax. Vigorously encouraged by the surrounding Arab radio networks, they pack and flee – 6,000 from Tiberias, 40,000 from Haifa; almost all the Arab population in Jewish-held areas departs, driven out or fearful. Here are already the makings of the great enduring emo-tional political factor of the whole Middle East: the Palestine problem of the homeless refugees – this is its conception; its gesta-tion is for the future.

The stage is now ready for the culmination of the story, of a sick and sorrowful conflict not between right and wrong, but between two forms of right and, maybe, two forms of wrong.

*By 1947 already the Arabs were growing uneasy,
even those so unpolitical they were not aware of
the cause of their unease. The panic had not yet
begun, but the exodus has. An Arab family leaves
Jerusalem, the father leading his donkey, wife
and children aboard the camel laden with their
goods, headed for somewhere safer than the
Holy City.*

THREE

By the spring of 1948 it was fair to say that no central government existed in all Palestine, no writ ran, no overall authority prevailed. The country was a shifting mosaic of contending overlordships. Armed Arab bands held the central Galilee; the Haganah controlled the east. The new Jewish administration had set itself up on the coastal plain, and the Jews dominated from Haifa to the Jordan. The British held on to all the enclaves from the seaport of Haifa to the airfield of Emek Zebulun, now protecting the lines of retreat for what was left of their civil government. An Arab area ran from Lydda to Ramallah; the Jews were on the banks of the Jordan and the northern Dead Sea. The most solid Jewish area ran from Zichron Yaa'qov to Rehevoth, with its firm centre in Tel-Aviv. For such a small country the military confusions were extraordinary.

The Jewish section of Jerusalem – New Jerusalem built outside the walls – was now surrounded on three sides by the Arabs, operating either on their own or with the help of British troops. The fourth side, to the west, that is to say the highway to Sha'ar Ha'Gai, was still controlled by the Jewish Haganah; it was by now the only means of access.

The northern Negev to Beersheba was no-man's-land. The British had withdrawn their army and police. Armed Arab and Jewish bands roamed to and fro; the outpost Jewish desert settlements were embattled and entrenched behind their defences. As May 1948 arrived it was clearly the stage before the last.

By now the land of Palestine was seeing the beginnings of the phenomenon later so familiar in so many parts of the world; the arrival of the vultures, first in groups of individuals landing from the sky with a rustle of cable-forms and typing-paper, later in flocks, wheeling round the stricken country, requiring unobtainable things, impatient for carrion. Such a description, though hard to avoid, is unfair to the erratic groups of the world's Press correspondents, who would demand with some justice to be defined not as vultures but as carrier pigeons. Many indeed were that; some could be held to be doves, and some even as parrots. Their presence in this tangled scene gave an extra touch of the bizarre.

Mostly they found themselves temporarily nesting in Tel-Aviv, as the one centre of some reasonable stability. They roosted in the group of hotels along Hayarkon Street by the sea: the Gat Rimmon, the Arnon, the Kaete Dan, a wildly congested establishment on whose site now stands the opulent Dan Hotel. Tel-Aviv is now Hiltonsville like everywhere else, but in the 1940s it was far otherwise. Tel-Aviv was (and it must be said still is) a town of almost stunning architectural charmlessness. Its visual crudity almost reached the sublime: a formless association of grey cement shoeboxes set up, one felt, at total random, a kind of frontier mining-camp petrified in solid form yet somehow at all times insisting on an atmosphere of prim suburbia. It was Golders Green in the Klondyke. It was a bit of Leeds with a Biblical hemline. Just as the serene honey-coloured loveliness of Jerusalem was a solace and enchantment to the spirit (though alas in recent years the glory is fast departing) so was Tel-Aviv a permanent nudge and a jostle and a raucous cry. Yet to say it was graceless is far from saying it was without attraction; indeed it had a kind of urgent thrusting beguilement, a frenetic sleepless stimulation that, once you had fallen for its mad cosmopolitan individuality, tended to hold you forever, though you were hard put to explain why.

Making every allowance for the increasing and by now oppressive shortages, the food in Tel-Aviv was grim indeed. What, one asked, had happened to the great traditions of the Jewish kitchens of Vienna, of Warsaw, even of Whitechapel; could it be that the art of Jewish food existed only in exile and had somehow evaporated when translated to the homeland? Where, in a word, had all the great kosher cooks gone? To which came the sad reply: 'A good cook is never persecuted; why should he leave home?'

Throughout Palestine the Mandate was visibly disintegrating. Since the passage of the UN resolution on the partition of the country, through the wholly unexpected and almost heretical alliance of the Soviet Union and America, and the pained British realisation that they were after all not to be asked to stay on, the Mandate had thrown in its hand with an abruptness that could almost have seemed petulant. The Chief Secretary's office (still, to the end, in the King David Hotel in Jerusalem) formally announced that the whole civil organisation, including the High Commissioner, would pack up on the 14th of May, and that the troops would be withdrawn shortly thereafter. Both the Palestinians and the Yishuv were deeply sceptical, but it certainly looked plausible.

The fact was, of course, that the Quit Palestine acceptance was just one phrase in an historical passage of vast significance that was already changing the face of the world, and within fifteen or twenty years would have transformed it: the end of Empire. It had begun the previous year with the independence of India; the tide of emancipation was beginning irresistibly to roll, had we only known it, throwing the Dutch from the East Indies and the French from Indo-China; by and by everyone, even the Portuguese from the land-mass of Africa . . . Palestine was a small and early part of the global process, but one more inevitable stage.

The British withdrawal from the Mandate was less decorous and dignified than the departure from India. The Mandatory Civil Service comprised British, Arabs and Jews, who had always worked together with a fair degree of co-operation under many forms of pressure; in spite of the tensions all around the apparatus had operated moderately well. But the British plan for departure, unlike their Indian scenario, had no provision for the transfer of institutions and public services to a successor authority. The administration of Palestine had already begun to fall apart. The Army under Sir Gordon MacMillan was profoundly tired of being the only British force in the world still being shot at two years after the end of the war.

32

The higher echelons of the Arab world well knew the causes of their anxieties, and sought the support of the British military command. They did not seek in vain. Here the Hashemite King Abdullah of Transjordan (right) greets Brigadier Edmond Davies, commanding the 9th Infantry Brigade, on the border between Transjordan and Palestine. Between them stands Brigadier John Glubb, the celebrated Glubb Pasha, British Commander of Abdullah's fighting force, the Arab Legion.

The British officials – many of them dedicated, with a lifetime of service – were faced with rootlessness. The Arabs foresaw it would now be a case of *sauve qui peut*. Especially did this apply to the Christian Arabs, the ablest and as a rule most senior officials: the impending Jewish State would be Jewish, whatever Arab State emerged would be Muslim; neither offered much joy to a gentile

33

He was not the Founding Father of Zionism, but he was the political begetter of the Jewish State – David Ben-Gurion, born David Green in 1886 in the Polish town of Plonsk. An immigrant to Palestine in the early days of the century, Ben-Gurion guided and controlled the Jewish struggle for independence, and Israel's transformation from a scattered tribe to an economic entity, and even a Middle Eastern power. He was Israel's first Prime Minister, and continued to be, with an interruption of only two years, from 1948 to 1963.

34

Dr Chaim Weizmann: a name greatly revered among the Jews, and among the scientists. Chaim Weizmann was a distinguished chemist who served the British Government well in the First World War by devising a process for the manufacture of acetone, a component of high explosive. It was he who extracted from Arthur Balfour, British Foreign Minister, the famous 'Balfour Declaration' of 1917 which declared

that 'HM Government viewed with favour the
establishment in Palestine of a national home for
the Jewish people.' When that dream became
real and Israel came into being, Dr Weizmann
was its first President.

of any colour. The Jewish officials, predictably, worked on a contrary plan, cleaving more and more closely to the Yishuv and Zionist directives. Mutual confidence had evaporated; the point was reached where Jewish and Arab officials searched each other on arrival at the office. By and by they ceased to come at all.

'When all allowance is made for frayed nerves and the weariness of long service in years of strain,' wrote Christopher Sykes in *Crossroads to Israel*, 'it does seem that after November 1947 an element of embittered cussedness, and the madness that goes with it, became a part of British policy.'

The British presence was symbolised by the High Commissioner, Sir Alan Cunningham, but he could not be blamed for its policy. Sir Alan was a dedicated professional British soldier, with all the honourable decencies and limitations that implies. He had not had the best of luck. He had led the East African forces triumphantly

into Ethiopia; he had commanded the Eighth Army in the Western Desert in 1941 and had been abruptly replaced. To be left the task of administering the conspiratorial imbroglio of Palestine was not perhaps what he could best have hoped for. For three years he contended as best he could, the sixth and last High Commissioner, with a vacillating and obstinate British Foreign Office that knew little of the nuances of this particular agony and still envisaged the Middle East in T. E. Lawrence terms, trying to come to terms with Arabs who deceived him and Jews who snubbed him, and subordinates who went their own way. He came increasingly to fear for the destiny of the Holy City, and was interminably rebuffed by those to whom it was supposed to be holy.

It is possible that there was no specific British intention to leave chaos behind them, but it is sure that no particular effort was made to prevent it. The British who had refused to co-operate with the United Nations in Palestine finished by not even co-operating with themselves. As for the Army, in its final days it was exercising authority only by force in local and disparate situations, independently and capriciously.

It seemed that the British were leaving with the prayer: *Après nous, le déluge*. They would depart; the Arab flood would sweep away the Yishuv; the British-led and British-managed Arab Legion of Transjordan would make short work of the settlements; Jerusalem would submit; the Jews, by then crushed on the coastal strip, would entreat Britain to return and save them, and the party could begin again untroubled by the past.

Meanwhile the Mandate would end on the 14th of May.

The Old Guard returns. In the winter of 1946 eight Jewish leaders, released from detention in the Latrun Internment Camp, returned to the Jewish Agency building in Jerusalem. Outside, a great crowd heard Moshe Shertok, director of the Agency's Political Department, say: 'Many difficulties still await us.' Here they made their reunion with Mrs Golda Meyerson (later to be Prime Minister Golda Meir) who had not been imprisoned. L to R: Moshe Shertock, David Hacohen, Mrs Meyerson, Mordechai Shatner, Itzhak Greenbaum and Dr Bernard Joseph, the Agency's legal authority.

FOUR

Over in Lake Success, where in those days the United Nations conducted its affairs, an extraordinary confusion had descended. Discussions continued in the Security Council, the Trusteeship Council, the General Assembly, and all the various committees that had been set up to debate the issues of a Palestine truce or trusteeship, a truce or a cease-fire in Jerusalem, a Mediation Commission; everything was put up, wrangled over, and lost. The endless argument seemed to have little bearing on the realities of the Middle East.

It was hard to remember how on earth the UN had contrived to involve itself in such a mess. Just five months before, when the fighting had begun in November 1947, more than two-thirds of the whole UN membership had agreed on the creation of a Jewish State in some form – including, miraculously, the US and the Soviet bloc. It had seemed at the time an unprecedented consensus of world opinion. Now the problems seemed to multiply. The UN Commission charged with liaison between the Mandatory Power and the prospective Provisional Government was stymied from the start when the British flatly refused to co-operate with it in any way; eventually it threw in its hand.

The Jews of Palestine had publicly rejoiced at the news back in November that the United Nations had formally voted for the initiation of a Jewish State. At the same time the Security Council got its first report from the UN Operating Committee on Palestine with its despairing rider: 'Only armed force will be able to enforce the Partition plan.'

But whose armed force? The Arabs had indeed endlessly threatened to oppose by force any sort of partition, but there was a tendency to believe – in the Jewish Agency as well as most other nations – that when it came to the crunch the Arabs would not really dare physically to combat a pronouncement of the highest international authority, that they could somehow be diplomatically pressurised to swallow it. It became clear almost at once that this was an illusion, and that for good or ill the Arabs intended to fight. What then could the fledgling world authority do about it?

There was no certainty that the UN's Charter gave it a legal right to send soldiers anywhere. There was even less confidence that any member-State would be in a hurry to provide them. Harry Truman had ruled out the use of US troops, and would certainly not stand for any sort of Soviet intervention in the Middle East. France was still a spent power, and wasting what energies she had in Indo-China and Algeria. Britain could obviously not be considered. None of the smaller nations had the slightest stomach for such an enterprise.

Moreover the United States itself was already beginning to back-track on its own Zionist concept even before it was born. The White House still supported the Partition principle, albeit with rapidly diminishing assurance. But the State Department's Middle Eastern division under Loy Henderson vigorously opposed it, as did James Forrestal's Defense Department. Both of them argued that it was all very well for Harry Truman to conciliate the domestic vote of American Jewry, but to antagonise the Arab States would be to open the Middle East to Soviet penetration and jeopardise US access to Arab oil. George Marshall, Secretary of State, was against the whole thing for the simple pragmatic reason that he believed the Jews stood no chance whatever, militarily or politically, and made it clear that the State Department was wholly opposed to US recognition of a certain loser.

The State Department prepared a long memorandum knocking down the Partition plan as inoperable, offering instead a complicated and wandering proposal for a ten-year Trusteeship for

Palestine, in some apparent belief that in ten years the insoluble problem would somehow go away. It was a memorandum of the topmost secrecy, which meant that every Palestine Jew of significance knew all about it at once, and great was the consternation thereof. There was already an American embargo on arms supplies to the Middle East; the British continued to arm the Arabs and blockade the Jews. The only hope now could be in the man who had supported the Jews so warmly up to now, and who after all was the single most powerful figure in the world: President Truman.

But by now, even Harry Truman had had enough. He had grown wholly tired of the perpetual Zionist pressures on him. He had also conceived a strong personal dislike of the main Zionist spokesman in the US, Rabbi Abba Hillel Silver, an importunate man who also happened to be an active Republican.

Among the Jewish settlers in Palestine there grew up a volunteer defence force, or militia, known as Haganah. At the most it numbered about 30,000 men. Over the years, discreetly based in the kibbutzim, it assumed the likeness and purpose of an army. Here a new draft of recruits parade in their uniforms for the first time at a secret camp near Tel-Aviv. They would go through an intensive ten-day course of training before being deployed into action. It was from Haganah that the more extreme National Defence Organisation, or Irgun Zwai Leumi, broke away.

Haj Mohammed Amin el Husseini, Grand Mufti of Jerusalem – Islamic religious leader and political activist, fanatical foe of Zionism, associate of Hitler during the Second World War. He was for a long time the focal point of Arab resistance to Jewish settlement in Palestine. Latterly there grew increasing rivalries and differences between the Mufti and the Military Committee of the Arab League in Damascus, which was organising the closing in of the Egyptian, Syrian, Lebanese and Transjordan Armies on the nascent State of Israel, and the Mufti's authority waned.

'The Jews are so emotional,' wrote Truman, 'and the Arabs so difficult to talk with that it is impossible to get anything done. The British, of course, have been exceedingly non-co-operative.'

President Truman felt kindly enough about the Jews, but he wanted no more impassioned and troublesome Israel arguments, and shut his office door.

As a last desperate resort the Jewish Agency sent for the failing old scholar who once before had attracted the President's sympathy, and even affection. But Truman turned even Chaim Weizmann down.

There then appeared in Kansas City, of all places, an individual of whose existence probably not one contemporary Israeli in a hundred is aware, but who may well have helped to initiate history – Eddie Jacobson, a haberdasher, a boyhood friend of the President, a not-especially Zionist American Jew. He happened to have once been in business with Harry S. Truman. With the greatest difficulty he persuaded the President to see Weizmann. It worked. The ageing and ailing Jewish scholar talked Truman back to his original way of thinking: the US would after all stand behind the Partition of the Holy Land.

But nobody told Warren Austin, the US delegate to the United Nations. Nobody told Warren Austin not to deliver his accepted State Department speech. Mr Austin therefore formally read out to the Security Council Mr Loy Henderson's proposals that Partition be abandoned.

Confusion grew more confounded. The Zionists fell to despair, the Arabs to rejoicing. President Truman was furious at the mess his own petulant dithering had brought about. The first complete U-turn of American policy had made the White House look foolish enough; a second one so soon would be preposterous. The President was wrathful at the State Department. Doubtless in Edwardian England he would have ordered someone to go out and govern New South Wales. Instead, he sent Loy Henderson to be US Minister in Khatmandu, Nepal.

In Palestine the killing continued.

The days of the Mandate were numbered, but the struggle went on. British troops go into action in the Yemin Moshe Jewish quarter of Jerusalem in an attempt to quell fierce fighting that had broken out between Arabs and Jews, and which lasted for six hours. One British soldier, six Arabs and a Jew died. An old woman crouches in the crossfire; a Jewish elder urges her to seek shelter.

43

At the outbreak of the fighting the Jews had been critically short of arms. The Haganah was still illegal – up to the very minute of British withdrawal the Army was still pursuing arms searches and confiscating caches of weapons.

To begin with the Jews had about 15,000 weapons: rifles, light machine-guns and a few three-inch mortars. This was from any military point of view a derisory armament. Far more would have to be bought – somehow. Much money would be needed. Golda Meyerson was sent to find it in America.

Golda Meyerson's fund-raising trip was a *tour de force*. She travelled throughout her old homeland demanding twenty-five million dollars. Every professional fund-raiser in the US said she was mad to ask for such a fantastic sum; Golda insisted it was an irreducible minimum and she would not return without it. Furthermore, protested the American Jews, funds raised by the United Jewish Appeal were customarily divided between Palestine requirements and the American Distribution Committee, and now here was Mrs Meyerson pre-empting the lot. Simple, said Golda Meyerson: raise fifty million and we shall split it, but the Yishuv must have its twenty-five million.

In two months Mrs Meyerson went home with twenty-five million dollars.

David Ben-Gurion was now in a position to send Ehud Avriel on a shopping-mission to Czechoslovakia to buy 25,000 rifles, 5,000 bren-guns, and something like fifty million rounds of ammunition, and anything else that came to hand, to be smuggled back into Palestine in careful degrees. The Jews, so hard pressed all winter, could not contemplate a measured and cautious offensive. The Haganah took on the Palestine 'Liberation Army' commanded by Fawzi el-Kawkji, a Nazi-trained freebooter and mercenary, and threw it out of Safad in the north. Then came Jaffa.

Jaffa was the wholly Arab town just down the road to the south of Tel-Aviv. It had, to be sure, been there a great deal longer than Tel-Aviv, and for a generation past had harried and assailed its Jewish suburb; in the 1920s the British gave Tel-Aviv its municipal autonomy, since when Tel-Aviv had swiftly grown in size and importance, if not in beauty. By and by a kind of no-man's-land had been created between the two, sandbagged and wired on both sides, with sharpshooters' points and fortified arms-stores. This had been a matter of regret for foreigners and the more broad-minded residents of Tel-Aviv, who had come to appreciate the greatly more interesting eating-places of Jaffa, and who were now tied to the more kosher austerities of the big new town.

But Jaffa in fact stood little chance; it was flanked to north and south by the Jewish areas of Tel-Aviv and Petah Tikvah. Only a narrow corridor ran inland to Ramleh and Lydda, and this was bitterly contested, since while Jaffa's communications depended on the western section, the survival of Jewish Jerusalem depended on control of the east.

Jaffa was finally strangled, despite the quite unconcealed efforts of the British to defend it on behalf of the Arabs. The British attitude in Jaffa was never completely understood, certainly not at the time; presumably some agreement existed between the Foreign Office and the Arabs that Jaffa should be protected while the Mandate endured; presumably the British did not want to see Arab Jaffa taken from under their noses by the Jews as Arab Haifa had been taken. It is almost certain that the British could have secured Jaffa against the Haganah and the IZL, but they could not secure it against the almost total desertion of the Jaffa population.

By the time we foreign observers saw Jaffa it was desolation; the Tel-Aviv border was smashed to dust; the Port area was lifeless, industries were crippled, the citrus fruit rotting on the trees, and 60,000 Arabs, virtually the whole population, fled.

The flights of the Arab citizens and villagers from their homes all over Palestine was the phenomenon of the time. There were as many explanations for this phenomenon as political attitudes in the region, but the happenings at Deir Yassin cannot be blameless.

Deir Yassin, an Arab village outside Jerusalem, had been attacked and taken in April by a trigger-happy combination of the Irgun and the Stern Gang in a crude massacre that was bloody and shocking and indefensible even by the brutal standards of the time, terrorism at its most savage, and an enduring black mark against the Jewish thug-element of its militant ranks. The atrocity

45

of Deir Yassin gravely shocked the majority of Palestine's Jewish community who, very properly, held it to be an outrage on Zionist ideals. Later the Irgun and Stern leadership was to deny the especially bestial excesses attributed to them by the very few survivors of Deir Yassin, but there is unfortunately much independent evidence that for a while the bandit-fringe of the Yishuv forgot its civilisation.

So Deir Yassin was certainly a factor in the Arabs' panic. So was the subtle Palmach propaganda spread in Arab villages that it might be repeated. Nevertheless even before Deir Yassin, or anything like Deir Yassin, the tranquil Plain of Sharon, where Jewish–Arab relations had always been neighbourly, was suddenly emptied of Arabs. The Arabs of Tiberias vanished for no evident reason at all, taking to the roads in their hundreds, clutching their possessions in boxes and sacks, jamming the thudding buses. After the fighting for Haifa the Jewish authorities and the British Major-General Sir Hugh Stockwell entreated the Arabs to remain, but they left nonetheless, piling into any craft seaworthy enough to take them to Beirut. When the Haganah occupied Beit-Shan they found it utterly deserted.

This exodus seemed more puzzling then than it does now. The rich Arab classes had prudently been moving out for months, leaving the masses in the towns without any leadership other than from the Arabic radio, which screeched doom daily. There was growing rivalry between the ex-Mufti of Jerusalem and the Military Committee of the Arab League in Damascus and the milling groups of independent Arab bands, most of whom – with the exception of the British-led Arab Legion of Jordan – were in the game for the loot, and until the time came to pillage the defeated Jews they practised on the local Arabs. All real Arab authority in Palestine was collapsing.

In days to come it became commonplace for the Jews to insist that it was the Arab leadership, especially in Syria, that instructed the Palestine Arabs to leave, telling them that when the British finally left they would return in triumph and take their recompense from the surviving Jews. The Arab leaders deny this, protesting that only thus can Israel shift the blame for the dispossession of

46

the Arab refugees. Both sides of the argument are, like everything else in this strange imbroglio, partly right and partly wrong.

The fact was that to the ordinary poor and unlettered Arab this was never a war between two States. It could not be, since he had been told all his life that the Jews had no right to a State. It was an endemic clash of communities, and it was far from new. Over the years when the Arab peoples of the Middle East had been dominant, Arabs had butchered Jews in Jaffa and in Hebron in the 1920s, Druzes had killed Christians, Turks had slaughtered Armenians. To the Islamic mind this had always seemed a reasonable enough state of affairs. The big difference now was that the logical victim was now most palpably fighting back, and might well be in a mood to take revenge for past wrongs. The cruel incident of Deir Yassin made this appear only too likely. The Arab Press and radio piled on the agony – hoping, perhaps, to fortify the resistance in Palestine. The result was the opposite: the terrified Arabs fled. The sorrow of the refugee camps was born, a challenge to the conscience of sensitive Israelis and an enduring political and moral weapon for the Arab Middle East.

It did however make things easier for the Jewish authority. There was no fear of an Arab underground resistance, no problems about divided communities. When the imminent State came into being it would at least be dominantly Jewish.

That is, if indeed it came into being – and up to a week before the deadline for the British departure that was far from a certainty. The surrounding Arab nations made no secret whatever of their intentions. In the south an Egyptian armoured brigade of 4,000 men was camped just across the border. Three regiments of the Syrian Army was ready in the north. The Lebanese Army was trifling, but it was standing by to enter Galilee. The Iraqis were moving a mechanised brigade towards the Palestine frontier to work with the Arab Legion, with heavy armour and artillery that the Haganah could never hope to oppose. This was not to speak of Fawzi el-Kawkji's 'Liberation Army' which, though no longer a coherent force after its drubbing in Safad, could still join with any Arab fighting column.

Against all this was now mustered a Jewish militia of rather fewer than 30,000. Of these a third had no weapons at all, despite a year of desperate improvisation and most ingenious smuggling on a very considerable scale.

This was, as far as one could judge, the situation on the morning of 12th of May 1948. One might not in fact have completely realised it in Tel-Aviv, sweating away in the damp heat of the Palestine spring, filling the coffee-shops, lining up outside the provision-stores. Food had long been rationed. Profiteering was abundant. The newspapers carried headlines on the fighting in the centre, the south, and the north. Three days and two nights remained of the British Mandate.

Martial law in the Holy City. The Jerusalem curfew was briefly relaxed, so that the people could emerge and seek food. A British soldier stands watchful with his jungle-machete in the Mea Sharim area, where lives a Jewish orthodoxy so strict it was to reject the authority even of the Israeli State, since it had not been signalled by the Messiah. In the meantime, they have the Tommy with the knife.

FIVE

The Jewish National Administration, the Minhalat Ha'am, was meeting in the office of the National Fund at 11 Herman Shapira Street in Tel-Aviv. This National Administration had been set up the previous year by the Zionist General Council: an Administration of thirteen and a National Council of thirty-seven. With the ending of the Mandate this was to become the Provisional Government and the Provisional Council of State. It was still technically illegal, since the British had banned the establishment of any Jewish State institutions so long as their writ ran, consequently the group was anonymous. That is to say, everyone knew every name on it but said nothing. It was led by the shock-haired zealot who had been born David Green in Poland and who was now David Ben-Gurion, accepted leader of the Yishuv, Prime Minister to be.

The meeting of the Minhalat Ha'am lasted thirteen hours. It heard from Mrs Golda Meyerson, director of the Jewish Agency's Political Department – the once-Russian former Milwaukee school-teacher who became Golda Meir, and herself Prime Minister nineteen years later – on her adventurous and abortive talks with King Abdullah of Jordan. She had taken the immense risk of a journey to Amman in disguise, gambling on the chance that the irresolute descendant of Hashemite desert sheikhs, protected by a British-run Arab Legion, could be persuaded to stay out of the impending war. A week or two ago the gamble might well have succeeded, but in the meantime there had been Deir Yassin, in the meantime the pressures from all the neighbouring Arab States were building up; the King was 'sad and nervous', said Golda Meyerson. They parted in useless and despairing friendship.

Then the Minhalat Ha'am heard from Moshe Sharrett (later to be Foreign Minister as Moshe Shertok) on his talks in America with the US Secretary of State, General George Marshall. But chiefly it heard a sombre analysis from Israel Galili, chief of Haganah, and Yigal Yadin, its head of operations – Yadin, the young sabra, who knew the Palestine terrain better than most, since he had dug so much of it up. He was a brilliant archaeology student at the Hebrew University, at least in the time he could spare from his operations with the Palmach guerrillas.

Galili and Yadin forecast that the Arab armies would not attack until the Mandate officially ended – almost in a matter of hours. But the Jordan Arab Legion had already assailed the Jewish settlement of Kfar Etzion, by Hebron, and anything could happen. Kfar Etzion was of enormous importance: its 400 or so inhabitants were the southern anchor of Jerusalem's defences, halfway between Jerusalem and Hebron. They had been attacked for months; now the Arabs had them under siege. The biggest convoy ever was sent to force through 200 tons of supplies and 135 relief defenders; it reached the settlement, but on the way back it was ambushed and destroyed at Nebi Daniel, a little way beyond the Pools of Solomon.

That and the destruction of Etzion itself was a disastrous blow. The settlement had in fact been militarily operational for several weeks, harassing Arab transport between Hebron and Jerusalem. The settlers had succeeded well enough to bring on themselves the wrath of the first Regular Army unit to move in on the Yishuv, the Jordanian Arab Legion, assisted by the British. Faced with professional armour and artillery the inhabitants of Etzion were overwhelmed without much difficulty; it was the first important Arab conquest. To the Jews it was a stunning blow, because Etzion was a truly pitiless butchery. Seventy Jews were killed, many of them after surrendering, many of them finished off most barbarously by Arab villagers instructed by legionaries. By the end of the Etzion day the massacre of Deir Yassin was indeed avenged.

51

By 1947 Britain was seeking not so much to cling to Palestine as to find a way out. Disengagement from colonial responsibilities has always been harder than maintaining them. In the Palestine Conference in London Ernest Bevin sat next to Arthur Creech Jones, the Colonial Secretary, and Dr Adan Sarcici, delegate from the Yemen. At the Foreign Office Bevin was surrounded by and much influenced by the traditional Arabists of British diplomacy; he had little sympathy for Jews and none for Zionism.

It appeared clear that the British military plan was for the Arab Legion – British-officered and commanded by John Bagot Glubb Pasha in the name of King Abdullah – to capture all the areas specified for the Arab State after Partition, and also to deny the Jews the Negev desert, which would ensure the British Army base at Rafah. To this end the British had equipped and trained the Iraqi division which was to invade at the Legion's side.

Someone later said of that meeting that it was the culminating moment in something that the tribe of the Yishuv, knowingly or unknowingly, had been preparing for seventy years, ever since the handful of families had moved their goods and themselves from behind the walls of Jerusalem to the sandy coastal plain and founded the Jewish village of Petah Tikva, and Motza on the stony hills of Judea. Since those days of the 1870s three generations of Palestine Jews had 'builded the house' almost stone by stone. If it were now to be lost, as was more than possible, it would never rise again.

But Tel-Aviv in 1948 was – as it still remains – a place rejecting this sort of romanticism; the mood was strictly realistic and pragmatic, and certainly no more so than among the quorum of elders of the Minhalat Ha'am. David Ben-Gurion set forth his assumptions in bleak terms. Whatever happened – a blockade, even a selective blockade against the Jews, or a polarisation of the Powers between the two sides – the Jewish forces were in for a dauntingly testing time, far worse than most of them realised. Ben-Gurion feared for the Jewish morale. To be frank, he said, the Jews had been spoiled up to now. They had won too many small battles. The Arabs had not succeeded in occupying any real centres – until now, this moment, when the Jews of Palestine were so visibly shaken by the news of the seventy dead in the Etzion bloc just stormed by the Arab Legion. There would be worse to come, far worse; inescapably there would be heavy and heartbreaking losses; could the Jews who had just been diminished by six million Nazi sacrifices face still more? Ben-Gurion was a bitter realist; he was unsure how the Palestine fighters, already growing slightly smug, would stand up to the moral test.

He was also concerned over the interrelationship of the various fighting arms. Ben-Gurion had a lingering belief in a British-style army, disciplined in a national unity rather than rooted in local defence: this the Jews did not have. The elite commando ranks of the Palmach quite clearly held themselves in special regard, even to the extent of operating as a private army independent of the Haganah, even occasionally plundering Haganah for arms, with their own special left-wing ethic stemming from the kibbutzim. They were flexible, resilient, unorthodox, brave; their independence was their strength. This had worked very well against an occupying Mandatory power; it could be anarchic in a war for national survival.

The 'security' or 'defence' organisation of the Yishuv had indeed for years been in a great patchwork of differences, of purpose and even of authority. For seventy years past Palestine Jewry had been dedicated to the dogma of self-defence: every new settlement founded created a nucleus of its own – the 'Hashomer' principle, originating in the slapdash old Turkish times with the 'Jewish watchmen'. Under a British administration, with a European theme, and, as everyone thought, the Jewish sympathies of the Balfour Declaration, the 'Hashomer' system was replaced by the area volunteers of Haganah. But the self-defence principle lingered on. Only settlements would be threatened. There were enemies all round, to be sure, but they were too disunited to attack the whole country, and if they did the country would have to be defended by 'the Government'. But now 'the Government' was not just, as ever, an alien Government, but potentially a hostile one, or at least visibly disposed to favour Jewry's enemies.

The Arab States all around refused to countenance the creation of a Jewish State; the best that even the moderates among them would concede was a certain Jewish minority autonomy. The Palestine Arab leaders' intentions could be inferred from their own immediate past: Haj Amin el-Husseini, the Mufti, and his colleague Fawzi el-Kawkji, had both worked in Germany for the Germans during the gas-chamber age, the solution that had not been final enough for them.

54

With the attack inevitable, Ben-Gurion was obsessed by the necessity of organising Jewish power, what there was of it, on explicit and regular military lines – something that had never been possible before, because the British Mandate made such a thing impossible, but simply had to be done now that the State was imminent. For Ben-Gurion the word 'State' had now no meaning other than an instrument of war. 'I can think of no other meaning now,' he said. 'I feel that the wisdom of Israel *now* is that to wage war, that and nothing else, that and only that.' For the first time in its history the Haganah would be forced to abandon the techniques of a clandestine resistance and become an organised army.

Yet even now, with the crisis upon them, the institutions of the Yishuv had no legal or coercive power. Their whole function was built on consent, consensus, coalitions, the maintenance of delicate opposing balances in a society where everyone then, as now, knew better than everyone else, every groupment wanting its pound of flesh, or maybe yet it would settle for fourteen ounces – a National Command and a General Staff, a Security Committee and an Agency Directive, a Mobilisation Campaign Directorate and a Mobilisation Centre for National Service ... David Ben-Gurion cut the Gordian knot and made himself Head of Security.

It produced a predictable row. Old volunteers of the secret armies accustomed to underground resistance methods resented the prospect of working to schematic military formulae. Many people and newspapers of influence denounced the proposal to replace the essential pioneer principle in Haganah and Palmach. It was said that Ben-Gurion's postulate of 'an army like other armies' was a disguise for his own intention to seize authoritative power.

Nor can it be denied that this was Ben-Gurion's wish. Yet in his mind authoritative power did not imply dictatorship; to him the crisis was so vast and the perils so immediate that someone had to decide something; as things were going the survival of any coming Jewish State could hardly be left to the quarrelsome Jews.

On that day, the 13th of May 1948, the issue was momentarily shelved and a very lonely Ben-Gurion brooded at the head of the Minhalat Ha'am.

*In November 1947 the General Assembly of the
United Nations by a narrow vote (from which
Britain abstained) decided that the only possible
solution to the Palestine impasse was Partition,
and* ipso facto *the legalisation of a Jewish State.
In the Assembly, not altogether concealing their
satisfaction, were David Ben-Gurion, then
Chairman of the Executive of the Jewish
Agency, and Dr Nahum Goldman, a member of
the Executive.*

*All over Jewish Palestine there was jubilation
at the United Nations' decision. In New York,
too, thousands of Jews danced the* horah *in the
streets. It was a moment of relief and pride for
Dr Chaim Weizmann (left) and Moshe Shertok,
chief spokesman of the Jewish Agency. Between
them is Mrs Weizmann.*

When the attack came, as it would in a matter of hours, the Jews would have about 18,000 armed men out of some 35,000 enlisted. They could invoke another 15,000 on the farms and settlements who had some kind of arms, but only for domestic defence. The women and children would have to be evacuated from the really vulnerable places – but where to? Nowhere in the country could be called safe, not even Tel-Aviv.

Yigal Yadin set out the imperatives. All the country's transport, public and private, must at once be placed at the disposal of the Army. Every Jew who had experience of foreign military service must enlist forthwith, no matter what work he was doing. Every firearm in the land must be nationalised.

The Arabs in Tulkarm were but ten miles from the sea; should they drive through, the Palestine Jews would be cut clean in half. The Arabs in Ramleh and in the airport region of Lydda were twenty minutes from Tel-Aviv. As far as anyone could see the Negev

Jewish Palestine went en fête *that November of 1947 when the UN announced its approval for the division of the country. In Jerusalem they danced all night; they crowded on to an armoured car driven by an almost-invisible British constable.*

Desert was completely open to any Egyptian armoured force. Apart from a few stolen three-inch mortars and some dubious home-made 'Davidka' cannon there was no Jewish artillery at all, and of course, not one operational fighting aeroplane. It was true that thanks to Ehud Avriel's beavering away with the new-found dollars plenty of arms were stockpiled in Europe, on airfields all over the world an extraordinary miscellany of old and nearly new aircraft was waiting, with a polyglot crowd of volunteer pilots and crews to operate them, but the whole array of equipment and men must needs stay where it was until it could be transplanted to a legally defined State. And by the time that came about it could well be too late.

The main strategy of the Haganah was evident: it would concentrate what forces it had where the first engagements were likely to happen; this meant forcibly ejecting potentially hostile inhabitants from their areas, and it had not always been very tenderly done. Already the Jeputhah Brigade had taken all the necessary parts of eastern Galilee, including the town of Safad, and were now waiting for the expected invasions from Syria and the Lebanon. The Golani Brigade was waiting around Beit-Shan for the Iraqis and Jordanians. The Alexandroni Brigade was around Nathanya, in the expectation that the Arabs would attempt to split the Jewish regions in half by cutting into Samaria or the Plain of Sharon. The Givati Brigade was to control approaches in southern Judea. As for the outlying settlements, their plight was full of doubt. Should the Egyptian Army or the Arab Legion decide to select anyone of them to reduce with artillery and armour its chances would be very small in the total absence of anti-tank weapons or any real kind of air support.

By now virtually no levies at all were left in Tel-Aviv.

There now remained less than two days to go.

The situation in Jerusalem was very bad. The Jewish commercial centre had been burned. The 2,500 Jews living in the Old City were wholly surrounded. The British continued to demand their evacuation, though with diminishing resolution, but no effort was made to impede the Arabs' activities. The trucks of explosives that blew up the office of the *Palestine Post* had been escorted through the Haganah roadblocks by British Army deserters. All the Jewish outer settlements were cut off.

Most important to the Jews was of course Mount Scopus, the high point where lay the Hebrew University and the Hadassah Hospital zone. This was now to all intents and purposes wholly isolated, since the only access ran through the Arab area of Sheikh Jarrah. Ever since the Partition the Jewish Agency had sent an armed convoy up the two-and-a-half miles through the Arab ambushes to keep the hospital supplied. During the previous months the little journey from the Street of Prophet Samuel to Mount Scopus had been comparatively uneventful. Then a dreadful disaster arrived.

The convoy, of trucks and buses and ambulances, bearing the red emblem of the Star of David, the Jewish Red Cross, and carrying with it among the hospital and university supplies a singular passenger-list of doctors, teachers and nurses, including the Director of the Hadassah Hospital, the celebrated optical surgeon Chaim Yassky, was almost through the Arab area of Sheikh Jarrah when it was mined, stopped, and destroyed. At least seventy-seven Jewish doctors and nurses and helpers were killed. So totally was the convoy burned out that two dozen bodies were never identified.

It is a memorable aspect of the closing days of the Mandate that the British, stationed less than a mile away, refused to intervene. In spite of desperate appeals from Colonel Jack Churchill, second-in-command of the Highland Light Infantry, who saw the carnage, the British Army remained immobile, arguing, perhaps rightly, that this barbarous ambush was an overt reprisal for the Irgun's equally atrocious attack on the village of Deir Yassin. Of such abominations were made the dying days of British rule in Palestine.

61

SIX

Meanwhile and until the last moment the wildly academic debates continued in the UN. Jerusalem's political status was unique. It was accepted that Palestine should be somehow or other divided, but Jerusalem was different; Jerusalem as a trebly Holy City was set apart; it had to be internationalised, pacified, isolated, though nobody really knew how. The British High Commissioner, General Sir Alan Cunningham, produced his truce proposals, which theoretically had much merit. But Sir Alan and the British Mandate itself were due to abandon ship in less than two days. How could he or anyone impose a peace on Jerusalem with the rest of the country at war?

The Minhalat Ha'am voted to reject the truce. To have accepted would have meant the postponement of the declaration of the State. This now meant that Israel would formally come into being in two days' time, to rule as much of Palestine as could be secured by force of arms. It was as simple, or as complex, as that. Everything in the short and troubled history of Israel has been the same.

Now that the UN's authority for a projected Jewish State was acknowledged, the bitterness of Palestine exploded into almost daily violence. The Palestine Arab Higher Committee ordered a General Strike, the Jewish Agency ordered all young Jews to register for 'Security Services'. Here, in the heartland of Jerusalem, Jewish firemen fight the blaze of civilian buses attacked by Arab incendiary mortars.

As the last hours slipped away life seemed only marginally changed in the Jewish city of Tel-Aviv. Since the crisis had closed in and the Palestine fighting had escalated half a year before, Tel-Aviv's street scene had somehow grown tauter, with undercurrents of neurosis; but then it had never been a tranquil town, any more than any Jewish *quartier* is a tranquil place, nor is it yet. The young had somehow evaporated – the most noticeable phenomenon one was to observe many times in the years to come, as the recurrent pull of emergency drew away potential soldiers from the streets to the camps – but the coffee-shops were busy, the streets rang as ever with polyglot argument. By now food was very hard to come by; there was a raging black market in almost everything. Tel-Aviv, with its back to the Mediterranean, could not possibly have the same sense of claustrophobic loneliness as Jewish Jerusalem; nevertheless there was a feeling of embattlement. The exit-roads out of Herzl Street and Allenby Street towards Jerusalem were blocked by Arab suburbs. The road from Hatikvah to Lydda airport passed through Arab villages; traffic to the south was obliged to follow

intricate roundabout routes. Yet businessmen and municipal officials went about their affairs much as before, though many of them were part of a part-time Emergency Committee. Three locations buzzed day and night: the Jewish Agency building on Nahlat Benjamin Street, the Va'ad Leumi office on Yehuda Halevi Street, and the 'Red House' by the sea at 44 Hayarkon Street, near the Kaete Dan hotel: that was the Haganah HQ.

The Va'ad Leumi occupied itself with organisational preparations for the State. The Jewish Agency was busy financing security and arms procurement. Haganah was obsessed with surviving the coming war.

In furious protest at the proposed Partition, Jerusalem Arabs turn on the neighbouring Jews, set fire to their homes and shops, and burn their possessions.

Meanwhile as the deadline grew nearer the weary meeting in Herman Shapira Street was still wrestling with tedious and legal problems of almost absurd complexity. What, in fact, were they to call themselves? The United Nations had laid down that its Palestine Commission would progressively transfer its powers to a Provisional Council of Government. But the British had refused to allow the UN Commission to enter the country, so it had no means of transferring anything to anybody. Nor could this *ad hoc* group in Tel-Aviv call itself a 'Provisional Council of Government', for the reason that the British, while having themselves virtually abandoned all authority, insisted that no other body whatever must even use the word 'Government', not until the High Commission had actually gone up the gangplank and left. The Arabs could come and go as they wished, Arabs and Jews could have pitched battles and set up administrations and commands, but not even in these last few hours could the word 'Government' be even tentatively mentioned without breaking the law.

The group temporarily named itself Moetzet Ha'am, or National Council. It was not worth having a new row at this stage.

Another problem was the Council's size. A body of thirty-seven was obviously too big and clumsy to run affairs efficiently. Yet here now entered the very Jewish factor of group-particularity and small prides. The Council had to be representative, and a baffling number of organisations demanded to be accommodated – Revisionists, Agudat Israel, Agudat Israel Workers, the Communists, communal groups of Sephardim and the Spanish, women's federations, the Jewish Farmers' Federation and the General Merchants' Association, the Chief Rabbis... It was daunting to realise how such a tiny land could produce such a multitude of contending factors.

Somehow or other a fairly compact unity of thirteen was conjured out of the mass. It left a residium of sulks that can be detected in Israel's affairs to this day.

Troublesome and obsessive considerations had for some time abounded. Not least was the profound concern: from where should the new nation be governed, where would be its seat of administration? 'Capital' was not the correct word, since the capital of

65

the Yishuv would forever remain Jerusalem, and in practical terms this is just where it could not be. But the new bureaucracy was already bursting at the seams; it had to have somewhere to go.

David Ben-Gurion had always longed for the State Centre, the Merkaz Ha'mdina, to be at Kurnub, in the Negev. Kurnub, not far from Dimona, had been a fortified city in the Roman-Byzantine age; it had once been irrigated and fertile and could be so again, though now it was little more than a Bedouin camp in a bleak and unpromising desert. Ben-Gurion's lifelong preoccupation had been the reclamation of the Negev wilderness by Jewish agricultural initiative. He also pointed out that a Government Centre were best established far from any border, and the Kurnub site was, in fact, the remotest from any potential frontier in any direction.

But the Jews did not control the Negev, and might well never do so. In the north the settlements were barely in touch with one another. South of Beersheba there was only a handful of Jewish villages; in the south-east Negev there was none at all. To establish a State Centre in Kurnub would have meant taking virtually all the Negev by force of arms and staying there, and this was manifestly impossible. David Ben-Gurion knew this and ruefully abandoned his proposition.

Golda Meyerson had her eye on Mount Carmel, which was also remote from frontiers, and a commanding site. But Haifa was to remain under British control until the last of their soldiers had been evacuated, and nobody wanted to start an administrative capital under the Mandate's guns.

When the news filtered out that the impending Government was in the market for a new Centre more offers came in. The village committee of Zichron Yaa'qov put in a claim: it was a pleasant place midway between Tel-Aviv and Haifa and it was one of the few hilly regions allocated to the Jews under the UN partition plan, so clearly the State's radio transmitters would have to be there; they could build a new port at Caesarea. Another offer came from the Council of Herzlia; it was named after the Founding Father, Theodor Herzl; it had a record of comparative tranquillity; it had plenty of seashore room.

The other alternative was the village of Sarona, just outside Tel-Aviv. Sarona was a German settlement built seventy-five years before by a Christian sect called the Templars, from Wurtemberg, which surprisingly was influenced by the appeal of Hitler in the 30s and sent its young men off to join the Wehrmacht. When the war broke out the remaining Saronites were at first interned, and then transferred to Australia. Thereafter Sarona had become a British police camp, heavily fortified, and known as the 'Bevingrad' of Tel-Aviv. When the British abandoned the Tel-Aviv region to the Jews, Sarona was taken over by the Haganah.

The Emergency Committee, faced with the immediate need for accommodating the first Free Jewish Government in 2,000 years, settled on Sarona. The problem then was to persuade the Haganah to move out. This was accomplished with the greatest difficulty. Everything seemed to be attended with the greatest difficulty. Sarona's water and electricity supply was hopelessly inadequate; there was not a paved road in the place. Every time the authorities took their eyes off the village homeless squatters from the battle-zones moved in, and had ruefully to be pushed out. Deep and stupid squabbles developed between the Emergency Committee and the Tel-Aviv Municipality, which claimed legal rights over Sarona, since it had bought the place from the British Custodian of Enemy Property and demanded to be paid by the Jewish National Fund. David Ben-Gurion thought this was absurd, since in next to no time the whole thing would be State property anyhow; furthermore he wanted any spare money the Fund had to be spent on arms for the coming war.

This fruitless dispute had only just been settled at the office of the Mayor of Tel-Aviv, when the impending Government agreed to split the village between itself and the Municipality.

Three days before the Provisional Government was due to come into being its new Centre still had no pavements, no mains water, no proper electricity. The offices had not enough furniture, and above all not enough typewriters, since Hebrew typewriters had never been particularly abundant. A workshop was established to change Latin-lettered typewriters into Hebrew characters, which in itself was not very helpful until the carriage could be made to travel from right to left. Departments of both the outgoing and incoming Governments complained bitterly, and began helping themselves to anything they could, until a Requisitioning Officer of the Haganah was set up to bring some sort of order back into a situation that was rapidly turning into a sort of anarchic bazaar.

Nor were these complications enough. Three days only before the assumption of his official Prime Ministership, David Ben-Gurion protested that he had received a letter from the General Manager of the Anglo-Palestine Bank arguing, not a matter of national finance or economics, but the recondite grammatical point that the Hebrew word *milveh*, or loan, was of the feminine gender according to Talmudic usage, though the National Administration's pundits had apparently ruled otherwise, and that he, the General Manager, was not going to put up with it. So a matter of hours before the final day Ben-Gurion had had to write to the head of the bank that the Talmudic vowelisation precedent was not determinative, since in fact the text of the Talmud was not vowelised anyhow, and so there.

The intricacies of that final Council in Herman Shapira Street can perhaps be remembered only by the exhausted members who sat it through. There were other questions. When the moment came, as it would so soon, would they proclaim a 'Government' or a 'State'? What would be its boundaries? It might be impolitic to proclaim a State without defining where it began and ended. Yet it was postulated that if the State were to be brought into being by force of arms, then clearly its frontiers would have to be determined the same way.

It is a piquant consideration that even at this eleventh hour, with the State clamouring to be born, nobody had finally decided what it was to be called. There were two choices: Israel, and Zion.

A sub-committee of Arabic experts reported that 'Israel' was acceptable in Arabic phonetics (as it would have to be). But the Arab countries had hitherto used the word exclusively to mean Jewish communities in Palestine; this might one day be prejudicial. However, 'Israel' it was, and that was the final decision of that long, long day.

Forty-nine hours were left.

68

In Egypt the Army prepares for what is already accepted to be the inevitable approaching war. Units of King Farouk's Bodyguard leave the Abdin Palace for the main Cairo railway station to take up positions on Palestine's southern front.

SEVEN

One enormous complication loomed over everything: the siege of Jerusalem. While these momentous decisions had to be taken, and the whole foundations laid for the first Jewish State for 2,000 years, Jerusalem – the whole focus and symbol of the Israel concept, Zion itself – was amputated from the body politic, isolated and helpless, its Jewish community denied food and the sources of water, communications and even information. The makeshift administration of the new country was, in fact, confined to Tel-Aviv and the coastal plain, almost wholly cut off from the City on the Hills.

This was much more than a sentimental handicap, for Jerusalem was more than a symbol. Almost all officials of practical experience and qualifications were up there – the members of the Mandatory Civil Service, the Va'ad Leumi, the Jewish Agency; Jerusalem alone had always been the administrative and political capital. The technical services were in Jerusalem, all the trained staff of the taxation machinery (of which the Yishuv in practice knew almost nothing).

The British Mandatory administration had by now suspended the collection of Income Tax. At the desperate request of the Emergency Committee the district tax-offices started work again, insisting on paying all their monies into a special account at the Anglo-Palestine Bank (soon to become the Bank Leumi Le'Israel) to protect themselves in any future enquiries. Everything else that

70

went to make up a reasonable Finance Ministry – Accounts Department, Budget Office, etc. – was out of reach in Jerusalem.

Moreover many useful experts who were not immured in Jerusalem had often vanished into the field. It had been a serious mistake, everyone now realised, to draft so many essential technicians into the fighting units; scores of experienced men were now dispersed in various armed corps all over the countryside and could not be reached.

One of those who had remained, however, was indispensable: Mrs Hannah Even-Tov, who had run the Jewish Agency's archive section. As the days of the Mandate ticked away Hannah Even-Tov's squad made it their business to rescue every piece and thing from Government offices vacated by the British or taken by the Haganah. In the final days this salvage brigade took into custody the presses of the Government printing-office, the equipment of the Public Works Department, the instruments of the Meteorological Office, the records of the broadcasting service, the legal library of the Law Courts and Land Registration records, every file and document that might help the transition from the old authority to the new.

Inside the city the pressures grew. The food shortage grew from the acute to the perilous. Dov Joseph, whom Ben-Gurion had appointed long before as Civil Affairs Chief for the Jewish community, reduced the week's ration to three ounces each of dried fish, beans, lentils and pasta, and an ounce and a half of margarine and four slices of bread. Children were allotted one egg a week. Haganah soldiers got three cigarettes a day.

A week before the Mandate was due to expire, every water-tap in Jerusalem suddenly dried up. At Ras el Ein, miles away, the Arabs had cut the Old City's water-line. The prescient Dov Joseph had foreseen this long ago, and for five months had been building up reserves in the Jerusalem cisterns – enough, it was reckoned, to allow the city to survive on a ration of two gallons daily per head, distributed in horse-drawn water-carts. In the heavy heat of a Palestine June, and for every purpose from drinking to washing and flushing the lavatories, two gallons a day was not much.

Brigadier John Bagot Glubb Pasha, British commander of King Abdullah of Transjordan's Arab Legion (in which he wore a Lieutenant-General's insignia) hears a report from one of his Bedouin privates on an encounter with Jewish forward posts in the Latrun region. Besides the Legion, three regiments of the Syrian Army were ready in the north, the Iraqis had a mechanised brigade on their frontier, 4,000 Egyptians were encamped in the south.

The situation in Jerusalem grew daily graver. The Jewish commercial centre had been burned out; all the Jewish outer settlements were cut off and besieged. The 2,500 Jews in the Old City were wholly surrounded, and could be supplied only from outside. Here a Haganah truck loaded with food starts from the Jerusalem Police Headquarters, headed for the beleaguered Old City. Two British constables with tommy-guns ride with the truck.

From the Jewish coastal plain to Jerusalem ran the road – the only road, forty-six miles of it, the road used by the Romans, Saracens, Crusaders, Turks, and now the most vital and dangerous highway in the country. It climbed at first gently from the Mediterranean through the citrus groves past the British military camp at Sarafand, and then it entered Arab territory at the old historic town of Ramleh. Soon the road began to climb the 2,000 feet towards Jerusalem; it entered a defile in the Judean hills, past the Trappist monastery of Latrun, the House of the Seven Agonies. The gorge narrowed, its walls grew steeper; everything passing through had to crawl in low gear under the gunsights of the snipers in the ruins of the Crusader fort of Kastel.

The groaning convoys of old Jewish supply vehicles, delivery vans, factory trucks, kibbutzim farm wagons, anything that would move, ran this gauntlet, with great losses. Without these ramshackle caravans Dov Joseph could have never kept Jewish Jerusalem alive.

Militarily, too, Jerusalem was a deplorably difficult place to organise, as the Haganah commander David Shaltiel was forever learning. The Haganah was perhaps weaker in Jerusalem than any- where else in Palestine. The British had been in a position to watch Jewish activities in Jerusalem most closely, and clandestine training had been extremely difficult. At the same time the Irgun and Zvai Leumi and the Stern Gang had always been strong in Jerusalem, and both these strong-arm organisations maintained a relationship with the Haganah that was both arrogant and suspicious. The Jewish Agency had, albeit reluctantly, accepted the principle of internationalisation for Jerusalem; Irgun and the Stern vehemently rejected it. In no way did they feel an obligation to co-operate with the Haganah; on the contrary they were prepared to loot and prey on Haganah arms and supplies as readily as on anyone else. Jerusalem too, was an intricate mosaic of ethnic communities and sects, many of them mutually hostile. The extreme Orthodox Hassidic groups who lived in the Mea Sharim and called themselves Guardians of the City vigorously opposed any sort of involvement with the resistance forces; many of the old rabbinical communities bitterly opposed the proposition of any sort of State of Israel that was not physically brought into being by Messianic dispensation.

(Many of them continue to reject the temporal authority of the State to this day, and great has been the botheration thereof.) These old religious scholars were relentless in their opposition to the Haganah, Irgun or Stern alike, insisting that the duty of the male youth in the schools was to recite the Scriptures and reflect on abstruse theology, not to scurry about usurping God's function with a gun. Whenever David Shaltiel was able to communicate with Ben-Gurion he protested to him that his task of organising a reasonable defence of Jerusalem was becoming impossible, especially while the 3,000 men at his disposal had responsibility both for the Jewish quarter of the Old City and the scattered settlements all around, and as long as the members of Irgun and the Stern Gang were in fact fighting an independent war.

Of the famous, or notorious, Palestine Police scarcely anything remained. The outgoing British had so far as possible disbanded it, sequestered its vehicles, destroyed its files. From the handful of officers and constables still left in police stations under Jewish control a nucleus was re-recruited, but the military call-up took precedence over everything. A new Emergency Order from the Central Command for National Service now enmeshed every man between twenty and thirty-five, and all deferments for whatever reason were suspended. Time was now running so short that the Chief Rabbinate had to make a special dispensation that recruiting offices and assembly camps could be kept open on the Sabbath day. (It was expressly recorded that this was not to set a precedent.) The disruption of normal life was immense. But then there had not been much normal life for a long time, nor would be for a long time to come.

Jewish Palestine was an increasingly lonely place, more and more isolated from the rest of the world. David Remez, who took over the Ministry of Communications and Transport, found himself in charge of virtually nothing of either. There was the port of Tel-Aviv, administered by the embryo Jewish Marine Trust. Jaffa was out of action altogether. Haifa harbour was still run by the departing British Army, whose final exit it would be. The railway ran for only the thirty-odd miles from Haifa to Hadera. Of international

Commander of the Palestine Liberation Armies
– the veteran Fawzi el-Kawkji: originally Lebanese, soldier with the Ottoman Army, professional spy for many causes, wearer of the Iron
Cross, profound admirer of the Germans, with
whom in Berlin he spent much of the Second
World War. He was appointed to lead the Arab
resistance in Palestine – much to the chagrin of
his bitter rival the Mufti Haj Amin. Fawzi now
addressed Arab villagers in northern Palestine.
'All is ready,' he said, 'the battle starts when
I give the word.'

76

air traffic there was none; one by one the airlines had closed their services to Palestine, and there was no Jewish airline of any kind. Towards the very end it was announced that the small landing-field at Haifa would be opened for civilian flights from the 16th of May; it would accommodate nothing bigger than Dakota-sized planes.

The mail was equally paralysed. Even before it quit the country the Mandatory Government had formally seceded Palestine from the Universal Postal Union at Berne, and so rigid was its boycott of the UN Commission it refused even to pass on this service. Yet if they had done so, there were still no ships or planes to carry mail anywhere abroad.

For foreign telegrams there was a submarine cable to Cyprus – but it passed through Alexandria and was therefore virtually in the hands of the Egyptians. Only by an extraordinary stroke of luck was a new channel devised. Six months earlier the Jewish Agency in Tel-Aviv had asked the Agency office in New York to investigate the possibility of finding some powerful radio transmitters that could be operated independently of the British authorities (since the principal Mandatory transmitters were at Ramallah, which was to be embodied in the Arab State). New York arranged for an engineer from RCA to go to Palestine and find out exactly what was needed. When he arrived, it turned out that not one of the political big shots of the Yishuv had the least technical knowledge with which to answer his reasonably complex questions, and the situation became somewhat preposterous, until someone of the Va'ad Leumi remembered a friend, a certain Zvi Friedberg, who was a radio-communications expert with the Iraq Petroleum Company's terminal at Haifa. To everyone's relief it seemed that Mr Friedberg knew all that was necessary about radio technology, and was able to explain the Agency's needs to the American RCA representative. The Committee then fell upon Mr Friedberg's neck and asked him to run the whole operation. Mr Friedberg said by all means, provided he was appointed Postmaster-General. He was at once appointed Postmaster-General.

It was too much to expect, however, that all this elaborate communications gear could arrive before the arrival of the State itself. It was therefore put to Israel Galili that the main Haganah military transmitter – 'Kol Israel', the Voice of Israel – should become the official State radio, when at last it could do its business openly and no longer underground, no longer chased all over the place by the exasperated British. It would be more efficient, if less exciting.

EIGHT

If the tiny administration of Palestine Jewry was twitching with argument and academic dissension the state of their enemies was, had they known it (and almost certainly they did) even more divided and confused. Almost every Arab nation was motivated by different purposes and different ambitions. The only thing on which the Arab League appeared to be of one mind was the rejection of the Anglo-American plan for a three-month truce.

It seemed that the Americans and the British had quite arbitrarily and loftily decided to divide their functions according to their respective diplomatic histories and interests: the Americans would look after the Jews and the British would handle the Arabs, since in Middle Eastern affairs that was the name of the game. America had millions of Jews, and the British were supposed to have this traditional affinity with the Arabs.

The notion of this truce found no favour with the Arabs, who were confident that when their own regular Armies entered the Palestine arena they would make short work of the Jews and, in the words of the C-in-C of the Arab Forces, the Iraqi General Ismail Safwat, 'exterminate and purge any Anglo-American imposition of a status quo'. The Arabs had had enough of the status quo; the more they were soothed and conciliated politically the stronger on the ground the Jews became.

Apart from that, everyone's reasons were different, and few of them had much to do with the Palestine Arabs. King Abdullah of Transjordan was already resolved to absorb the Arab part of Palestine as part of his very considerable territorial ambitions, and his British patrons had raised no eyebrows at this. Abdullah controlled what was by far and away the most powerful and efficient Arab military formation, the Arab League, now inspired, trained, armed and officered by the British. The one thing in the world Abdullah desired was to become King of Jerusalem, than which in the eyes of Islam nothing could be more prestigious. His father had been kicked out of there twenty years before by King Abdul ibn-Saud, which gave him no love for the Saudis. King Abdullah had already denounced the Syrian Prime Minister Jamil Mardam for not keeping his armies up to scratch; there was equally little love between Amman and Damascus. The Lebanon had, as ever, little interest in anything other than business as usual.

There were also undisclosed differences between Abdullah and his own army. Glubb Pasha, head of the Arab Legion, was a loyal and dedicated Arabist, but he was also an Englishman, and he had been quietly recommended to limit any advance he made to the 1947 partition line. He commanded some 7,000 men, of whom 4,500 were front-line mechanised troops, led by British officers experienced in the Western Desert and in Germany. It was the most powerful striking force in the Middle East.

But Glubb Pasha had no especial ancestral feeling for Jerusalem. John Glubb was a *bedou manqué*; his men were bedouin from the desert, soldiers of space and movement; he had no wish to risk them in street-fighting against the doubtless urbanised and wily Jews. Glubb Pasha had no intention of destroying Jerusalem to produce its ruins for Abdullah.

Then there was the pale-eyed and high Machiavellian Mufti, Haj Amin el-Husseini, even more eager to return to Jerusalem than Abdullah. He was still the leader of most Palestine Arab forces. He knew of King Abdullah's plan to take over Arab Palestine and Jerusalem when the Jews were eliminated; if that took place there would clearly be no return to Jerusalem for him.

80

With Jerusalem under siege and blockaded, isolated and helpless, the only way to bring food
and relief to the city was by armed convoys up
the long and perilous road from Tel-Aviv to the
hills. Armoured cars manned by Haganah troops
escorted the trucks on the heavily-ambushed
road. Many left Tel-Aviv for Jerusalem; many
never arrived.

81

Down to the south in Egypt the young King Farouk now wore his Field-Marshal's uniform by day in the palace and after dark in the night-clubs. He had now enjoined his Prime Minister, Mahmoud Nakrashy Pasha, most doubtfully and reluctantly to declare war on the still unborn Jewish State. Two Egyptian brigades of some 15,000 soldiers were already standing by at El Arish, in the Sinai. An obscure Sudanese Colonel of the line called Mahommed Neguib offered the warning that but four battalions were in any way provisioned or prepared for action; he was reprimanded for his pessimism.

The newly formed Military Committee was established in Damascus; all Arab States agreed to contribute funds and arms. It named as its Commander an emotional General Ismail Safwat; he was an Iraqi, and therefore a family supporter of the Hashemite dynasty in Jordan and Iraq, which was equally loathed by the Egyptians, the Saudi-Arabians, and the Mufti. The promised arms and funds were sent to almost everybody except him. Local battle commands were distributed according to regional pull and family loyalties. It was in a high state of mutual suspicion that the Arab League met in Cairo.

What was now quite evident was that the Palestinians could not make any sort of impact on the situation by themselves. In their hearts the senior Arab statesmen had probably hoped that the 'Liberation Army' of Fawzi el-Kawkji could have demoralised and mastered the Jews with no more than their encouragement, but el-Kawkji's bands had been unexpectedly and seriously drubbed on the Plain of Esdraelon.

There was but one navigable road from Tel-Aviv to besieged Jerusalem, and it was open to ambush almost all the way. The Arab road block at Bad el Wad destroyed many Jewish supply convoys. The surrounding hillsides gave ample and easy cover for Arab snipers.

'Liberation volunteers' were drying up fast since Deir Yassin and were now irretrievably on the run, the Palestine Arabs were melting away. It was now clear that if the threatened Israeli State was to be put out of business in its infancy the regular Arab armies would have to do it.

It was equally clear that the Hashemites of Jordan and Iraq would dominate the post-war region unless the other Arab States did something about it. Abdullah's Arab Legion was incomparably the strongest Arab force, with its British arms and its British leadership; so too had the Iraqis been pledged all necessary British equipment for their assault on the Yishuv. For the Egyptians and Syrians to dither now would merely be to see their slice of the cake go by default.

At no time did it occur to the Arab high commands that they would not eliminate Jewish resistance in days, if not hours. Their dilemma was how to co-operate in this simple operation with the least disadvantage to their own individual interests.

The plan existed. It provided for the Syrians and Lebanese to march south to Nazareth while the Jordanians and Iraqis moved west; together they were to drive into Haifa. The Egyptians would come up from the south and take Jaffa and Tel-Aviv. The Jews in Jerusalem could be left meanwhile, besieged and encircled and soon to submit. If at any time there were a Great Power intervention, it would improbably be to their disadvantage.

Meanwhile, everyone saw their advantage differently. The Iraqis and Transjordanians envisaged the change of broadening the territory of the Hashemite family into at least part of Palestine, even if it meant coming to an arrangement with the Jews. Egypt saw the coming fight as a useful diversion for its own internal discontent. The British hoped to regain a fading power. The Jews of Palestine, themselves in a paradoxical way the godchildren of imperialism, would be fighting an anti-imperialist war, that was more and more becoming an inescapable war of survival.

Up to the last minute the Arabs were shifting their administration. The Iraqi General Ismail Safwat was eased out of his job as Supreme Commander to make room for King Abdullah. Accepting Abdullah even as technical Supremo was a bitter pill, but his troops were far stronger than anyone else's, and also closer to the front; moreover it was he on whom the British lavished their patronage. It would be no use anyone else seeking other foreign sponsors: Russia and America seemed already committed to the Jews, and France was meaningless. As a clincher, Abdullah observed that were he not so appointed, his Arab Legion would do the job on their own. For the time being, let Abdullah have his way; he need not live forever.

One Jewish armoured truck that failed to reach Jerusalem. At the outskirts of the city, in the Sheikh Jarrah quarter, the Arab snipers got it. They shot the driver fifty times through the slits in his armour-plate; they dragged his body to the roadside and left it, and the truck, to burn.

NINE

On that Friday, the 14th of May two separate and momentous acts were taking place in the divided regions of Palestine. They were an hour and a half's drive from each other, but they might have been in separate nations. In Jerusalem the British were moving out; in Tel-Aviv the Jews were moving in. That is to say the formal gestures of both acts were being performed, with some courtesy and ceremony, in the certain knowledge that within hours a wholly predictable and bitter conflict would supersede it all; it was like the punctilious ritual before an ancient Oriental duel. But now it was not the adversary who was presenting his courtesies to the coming State before departure; it was the referee.

At eight o'clock that morning Sir Alan Gordon Cunningham, High Commissioner of Palestine, left Government House in Jerusalem, wearing the field service uniform and insignia of a full General of the British Army. He saluted his guard of honour, climbed into his car and left the seat of the British Palestine Administration forever. The Union Jack came down, and up to the masthead run the flag of the Red Cross.

The night before he had broadcast his goodbye:

It is not my wish at this period of the British departure to turn back the pages and look at the past. It would be easy in doing

86

so to say sometimes 'Here we did right', and no doubt at other times 'There we did wrong'. The way ahead has not always been clear, the future has often been obscured. We have experienced great sadness in the past years, a sadness that much could have been accomplished and had to be left undone. But in our hearts will remain the constant desire that goodwill and amity may be established between us, one day...

He had not secured what he had most earnestly sought: the truce in Jerusalem itself. He had gone to Jericho to argue it out with Azzam Pasha of the Arab League and had indeed persuaded him to a cease-fire. The Jewish Agency had agreed to send Golda Meyerson to discuss it with him, and she had not turned up. Again the Jews had let him down. Now he was leaving Jerusalem an open prey to the fighting that was bound to begin at any moment.

Sir Alan Cunningham drove to the landing-field at Kalandia north of the city, climbed into his plane and flew to Haifa. There would be no next year in Jerusalem for Sir Alan ever again.

In Jerusalem no government of any kind remained. Field HQ had moved out two weeks before; nothing remained but the two field columns now moving out for good, one through the Sheikh Jarrah quarter of Jerusalem, north to Ramallah to swing south-west to the Latrun monastery crossroads, where a tank squadron had been shelling the Jewish forces at this vital intersection to pin them down and prevent any premature battle breaking out ahead of the convoy. When the British column was past the tanks packed up and followed on; whatever happened now was no affair of theirs.

The other column drove south through Bethlehem and Hebron, heading for the desert.

It was thirty years and five months after General Allenby's army had first entered the Jaffa Gate, and it was all over now.

For days, weeks, even months the local command of the Haganah had been preparing the tactical orders for what would have to be the almost instantaneous takeover of the vital sectors of Jerusalem vacated by the British – areas, streets, buildings, even corridors and rooms. It was imperative that the least possible time elapse between the physical departure of the British and the physical entry of the Jews; there could not be any vacuum or the advantage would be lost. To that end almost every yard of Jerusalem to which the Haganah had access had been surveyed and reconnoitred – alleys, cellars, rooftops. There had been innumerable rehearsals and run-throughs; the Jews had learned to move about Jerusalem as treetop animals move through the forest. There had been evolved an intricate system of temporary telephone communications and signals. Every neighbourhood commander knew, in theory, exactly what to do when the moment came.

For this, however, it was necessary to know precisely when the moment was to come, the time of departure of each British unit, military and civil, and its accurate route of departure. The Mandatory authorities had reasonably enough been fairly secretive about this, and a great deal of casually misleading information had been spread around. Yet the paradox remained that throughout the bloodshed and bitterness several pockets of good relationships, even friendships, had endured between British and Jew, and David Shaltiel's men were not without their contacts. They were also helped in no small degree by the British deserters who, bored or exhausted by the Army, or driven by some compelling love-affair, had quietly slid off into the arms of one side or the other, occasionally the Arabs but, not infrequently, the Haganah, bringing with them the occasional welcome weapon and ammunition, and also useful information for the Haganah's military intelligence.

So by that Friday dawn when the British Administration was moving into its last phase in the Alamein and Allenby Barracks, in Bevingrad and Notre Dame and the Hill of Evil Counsel and the King David Hotel, they were not unobserved. And from both sides.

Within two hours of the British departure the Jewish task-forces had moved into most, though not all, of the prepared objectives; they occupied the Post Office building, the Russian Compound, the former Police HQ, the Notre Dame complex and the telephone exchange, a most important psychological advantage.

The Arab League meets in session in Cairo to consider the coming offensive to fight against the Partition of the Holy Land. The chairman, in the tilted tarbush, is the Lebanese Prime Minister Sa'adullah Jabrilnat. To his left, Hamdi Pashashi, Iraqi Foreign Minister; to his right, Said Pasha Mufti of Transjordan. It was February 1948. D-Day was not far off.

In the Valley of Ajalon, where Joshua had fought the Canaanites, the Haganah was pressing up to Latrun. Another column had by-passed Acre and reached Nahariyah, moving on to the Lebanon border. For a time it seemed as though everything was going well.

Except, of course, that ten miles south of Jerusalem the remnants of Kfar Etzion were finally reduced to ruin; the handful of survivors were going into captivity in Jordan.

Everybody was winning; everybody was losing.

The next day would be Shabbas: Saturday, the Sabbath. Whatever had to be done in Tel-Aviv must be done before the shofar sounded at sundown, even something as extraordinary and unprecedented as the creation of a nation.

Until the last days there was some doubt as to where the big deed would take place. The best and most appropriate setting had seemed to be the Habimah Building on Rothschild Boulevard, but it was conspicuous and predictable, and it was feared that it could well be attacked from the air if it were made known what was to take place. It was decided to move the ceremony down the road.

The invitations were sent out by Zeev Sharef, Secretary to the Administration, and later to the Cabinet.

'We have the honour to invite you,' it said, 'to the Session of the Declaration of Independence, which will be held on Friday, 5th Iyar 5708, 14th May 1948, at 4.00 pm in the Museum Hall. We urge you to keep secret the contents of this invitation and the time of the Council meeting.'

The guests were asked to wear 'dark festive attire'.

The document was signed by nobody.

The Jewish armed organisations had a long tradition of women soldiers. Here on the roof-top of a Jewish house in the Manshiah quarter of the Tel-Aviv–Jaffa complex, endlessly disputed, members of the Irgun engage the Arabs across the street frontier.

At last comes the day. In the Museum Hall in Tel-Aviv, on the 14th of May 1948, David Ben-Gurion, first Prime Minister, declares the birth of the new State of Israel. Under the portrait of Theodor Herzl, patron saint of Zionism, the National Council presents itself. L to R: *Baroch Shitrit, Police Commissioner; David Remez, Communications Minister; Fritz Bernstein, Minister of Trade and Industry; Felix Rosenbluth, Minister of Justice; Rabbi Judah Fishman, Commissioner for Jerusalem; David Ben-Gurion; Moshe Shapiro, Director of Immigration; Moshe Shertok, Foreign Minister; Eliazar Kaplan, Treasurer; Moshe Ben Tov, Minister of Public Works; Aaron Zisling, Minister of Agriculture.*

The Charter of Independence, and the man who brought it into being. The Proclamation of the State of Israel is triumphantly brandished by an official beside the strangely impassive profile of David Ben-Gurion, now its Prime Minister.

In Rothschild Boulevard in the middle of Tel-Aviv stood the Museum Hall, a building as undistinguished as all others in the town; it had once been the home of Meir Dizengoff, first Mayor of Tel-Aviv. It was to be undistinguished no longer.

Outside the hall was drawn up a guard of honour of cadets from the Jewish Officers' School. A strong detachment of Haganah military police meticulously scrutinised the credentials of every soul entering up the steps from the Boulevard. In the steaming heat of that afternoon the atmosphere of crisis was almost tangibly neurotic. The Yishuv had waited six hundred generations for this day; Jewry had trod a long hard road from Babylon and Pharaoh's Egypt and the deserts and the ghettos of the world; what had seemed endless was now at last to have an end. The moment could not and must not be wrecked now by a chance intruding enemy. Security was tense. Every arrival passed the cordons of guards who were men from Berlin and London and Cracow and South Africa and Iraq and Egypt, from the death-camps of Germany and Poland, from the farms of Galilee. No museum had ever been harder to enter.

The hall was crowded to suffocation, the heat magnified by the film-camera lights, the shadows broken by the flashbulbs. Above it all, against the blue and white hangings, looked down the portrait of the sombre-bearded Viennese journalist Theodor Herzl, who had dreamed it all – how long ago? Just over fifty years.

Below the portrait of Herzl sat the eleven of the National Administration and the secretary. At the centre table sat the fourteen members of the National Council. Around them in a semi-circle were the Rabbis, Mayors, elders of the Yishuv, officers of the Haganah command, councillors, fund-raisers, the Zionist General Council. But from Jerusalem none could come, nor from Haifa and the north. Tel-Aviv was still an enclave in a hostile land.

At exactly four o'clock David Ben-Gurion, wearing a necktie for the only time in living memory, rapped his gavel on the table. The whole hall rose to its feet. The Philharmonic Orchestra concealed upstairs drew up its bows – but they were too late, already the crowd was singing the 'Hatikvah'.

The end of an era. At midnight on the 14th of May 1948 the British Mandate of Palestine ended, and the State of Israel was born. Hours before, the High Commissioner Sir Alan Cunningham left Government House in Jerusalem. His standard was struck, a piper played him from the gates. His convoy left Jerusalem for the last time past a guard of honour with dipped regimental colours.

It faded out, and Ben-Gurion said: 'The land of Israel was the birthplace of the Jewish people. Here their spiritual, religious and national identity was formed. In their exile from the land of Israel the Jews remained faithful to it in all the countries of their dispersal, never ceasing to hope and pray for the restoration of their national freedom.'

His white woolly halo danced, his face glistened in the heat, his eloquence mounted to a Hebraic fervour; he was speaking for Joshua and David, Nehemiah and Ezra the Writer, for the fugitives from the Crusaders and Saladin and Spain, for the survivors of Dachau and Ravensbruck, for the sabra Yishuv who had drained the Hulah swamps, the founders of Rehovot, the builders of Tel-Aviv itself, for the immigrant bus-drivers and the waiters in the cafés of Dizengoff Square, and those who were yet to come.

'Therefore by virtue of the natural and historic right of the Jewish people to be a nation as other nations, and of the Resolution of the General Assembly of the United Nations, we hereby proclaim the establishment of the Jewish nation in Palestine, to be called the Medinat Yisrael: the State of Israel.'

It was far from over; he had now to read the Articles arising from the declaration, the setting up of provisional authorities, the principles of 'social and political equality of all citizens distinguishing not between religions, races or sexes, providing freedom of religion, conscience, education, language and culture, the safeguarding of the Holy Places of all faiths.

'We appeal to the United Nations for help to the Jewish people in building their State, and to admit Israel into the family of nations. We offer only peace and friendship to all neighbouring states and people . . .'

And finally: 'With trust in God, we set our hand to this declaration, at this session of the Provisional State Council, on the soil of the Homeland, in the city of Tel-Aviv, on this Sabbath eve, the fifth of Iyar 5708, the fourteenth day of May 1948.'

It had taken exactly thirty-two minutes. Plus, of course, 2,000 years.

The last salute. General Sir Alan Cunningham, final British High Commissioner, looks back from the launch taking him from Haifa to board the cruiser Euryalus, *bearing him away from a vanishing Palestine, and an infant Israel.*

Overleaf: *the first Zionist, and the Founding Father of the State. Dr Theodor Herzl, Viennese journalist, who created the concept of the sovereign Judenstaat in the Promised Land of Palestine. He called the world's first Zionist Congress in Basle in 1897. It took 51 more years for his dream to come true.*

EPILOGUE

And no one lived happily ever after.

Three times in the last quarter-century I have personally seen the endless tensions of the Middle East build up their content of hate and fear until it burst across the Israel–Arab borders, in one direction or another, leaving its predictable residue of triumph and defeat and sorrow and recrimination, solving nothing. Each time the world knew uneasily that the next time would be worse, and it was. Each time the wounds were deeper and the scars more brutal. Each time the world protested that this could not go on, while perpetuating the factors that made it inevitable. Each time one's heart sank a little more – not just for Israel, not just for Palestine, but for us – which is to say all of us. In this context, nobody has been very clever, and some have been very cruel.

By and by a new generation will grow up in the Middle East, both Arab and Israeli, which will reject the role of pawns in the Power Game, refuse the importunities and persuasions of the strong and cynical, and recognise, as many voiceless patriots already recognise, that what is done is done, and that both sides must make a future together, if there is to be one at all.

Amen.

INDEX

DATE DUE	

GAYLORD   PRINTED IN U.S.A.